n Centre

Working Together to Cut Crime and Deliver Justice

A Strategic Plan for 2008-2011

Presented to Parliament by
The Secretary of State for the Home Department
The Lord Chancellor and Secretary of State for Justice
The Attorney General
By Command of Her Majesty

November 2007

Cm 7247

£13.90

CONTENTS

PREFACE

Home Secretary
Jacqui Smith

Lord Chancellor and Secretary
of State for Justice Jack Straw

Attorney General
Baroness Scotland

As the three Ministers responsible for the Criminal Justice System in England and Wales, we are pleased to present our Strategic Plan to 2011. The Plan describes our vision for a Criminal Justice System which:

» is more **effective in bringing offences to justice,** especially serious offences;
» **engages the public** and inspires **confidence;**
» puts the **needs of victims** at its heart; and has
» **simple and efficient processes.**

It defines how we aim to achieve the vision, identifying how criminal justice agencies – police, prosecution, courts, probation, prison and youth justice services – will work together with other partners to improve efficiency and effectiveness in bringing offences to justice. It also sets out how the Criminal Justice System supports Government's wider drive to make communities safer through reducing crime and re-offending, as detailed in the Crime Strategy: *Cutting Crime: A New Partnership 2008-11*, published on 19 July. It sets the scene for the new Reducing Re-offending Strategic Plan which we will publish in Spring 2008.

The Plan was drawn up with the help of front line staff, practitioners and many stakeholders with experience of the Criminal Justice System.

The success of Local Criminal Justice Boards in delivering most of the commitments in our 2004 Strategic Plan has given staff throughout the Criminal Justice System confidence that agencies can work together to improve the service they provide. There is a shared determination by all the agencies to go further and address some of the tougher challenges which have emerged. Whilst we have made great strides in tackling volume crime, there is more to do to tackle some of the most serious crimes, such as sexual and violent crime and support the victims of these crimes. At the other end of the scale, we need to intervene earlier and more effectively with young people at risk, both victims and offenders. We will be working together with the Secretary of State for Children, Schools and Families, Ed Balls, and over the next few months coming up with further proposals to secure our ambitions for youth justice in the Children's Plan and the Youth Crime Action Plan.

We also need to continue our drive to tackle some of the most intractable problems – mental health, substance misuse and social exclusion – which underlie many crimes. We must focus the expertise of the Criminal Justice System on these serious challenges.

In meeting the challenges, we recognise it is crucial to take the public with us – inform them, consult them and tell them how we are responding to their views. We need to bring the Criminal Justice System closer to the people it serves. Local Criminal Justice Boards, working with local communities and local partnerships will have a key role in achieving this.

In doing this, we need to go further in improving the efficiency of every part of the system. We need to make better use of the technology that is now in place, and give local areas the freedom to innovate and drive locally-tailored programmes of change. There are promising signs that this challenge is already being taken up in many parts of the country.

The programmes of work we set out in this Plan are designed to support the local approach. Through our Beacon Approach, we are designing a blueprint for local leadership. The blueprint will enable boards to implement a co-ordinated programme of reform which achieves tangible improvements across the criminal justice agencies. Engaging effectively with local communities is a core feature, working through the neighbourhood policing, community justice and other programmes. Through community justice, we will continue to develop our problem-solving focus on both the offence and the offender and work in partnership with others to tackle underlying problems. Through this and our drive to improve compliance with the orders of the court, we will help to reduce the risk of re-offending.

We have set ourselves a challenging target on asset recovery – recovering double the amount in three years, sending a strong signal that crime does not pay. Offenders will also be held to account for their actions and we will offer them more opportunities to make amends to their victims and society. Working with local boards we will ensure that standards of service to victims and witnesses are embedded throughout the Criminal Justice System and that we respond to the needs of all victims, particularly the victims of the most serious crimes.

We will continue to drive improvements across the whole criminal justice process. But we will do so in a different way. At a national level we will provide the framework and support, but improvements will be driven at local level, informed by local priorities. We will measure and respond to the views of local people about their local services. We will work in partnership with local community and voluntary organisations. We will build on what works to make a sustainable difference to reducing crime and re-offending in communities. And staff at all levels will be supported and empowered to engage with their communities.

Home Secretary,
Secretary of State for Justice,
and the Attorney General.

CRIMINAL JUSTICE STRATEGIC PLAN 2008-2011: EXECUTIVE SUMMARY

This plan sets out how the agencies of the Criminal Justice System (CJS) in England and Wales will work together to build on the successful delivery of the commitments set out in our 2004-08 Strategic Plan and deliver a justice system which:

» is **effective in bringing offences to justice,** especially serious offences;
» **engages the public** and inspires **confidence;**
» puts the **needs of victims** at its heart; and has
» **simple and efficient processes.**

To achieve this, criminal justice services – police, prosecution, courts, probation, prison and youth justice services – will need to work more closely together through their Local Criminal Justice Boards (LCJBs) and other local partnerships to deliver efficient and effective criminal justice services. This will also support the Government's wider crime reduction and re-offending strategies to make communities safer, as set out in our new Crime Strategy: *Cutting Crime – A New Partnership 2008-2011,* published in July 2007.

The Criminal Justice System supports this wider agenda in the following ways. Through **efficient** services that make best use of resources, expertise and technology, the Criminal Justice System can free up the police to tackle crime and reduce fear of crime through visible policing. Efficient services also help to increase the satisfaction of users of the Criminal Justice System, especially victims and witnesses and therefore confidence of local communities more widely. A focus on efficiency also enables criminal justice agencies to be more **effective** in processing the more serious cases by freeing up the capacity to give the more complex cases and intractable problems the time they need. By focusing on both the offence and the offender and taking a **problem solving approach** – such as with domestic violence courts – the Criminal Justice System contributes to the government's wider target to **reduce re-offending.** Reducing re-offending cannot be tackled by criminal justice agencies alone: we need a range of partners to help us access the support offenders need to reform. This reduces the pressure on the Criminal Justice System by reducing the likelihood of offenders coming round the whole system again. A strong focus on **supporting victims and witnesses,** especially victims of serious crime, supports government's wider harm reduction and public protection aims. Above all, to build **public confidence,** the Criminal Justice System needs to inform, consult and involve local communities, account to them on performance and how the Criminal Justice System is responding to local concerns. To do this, delivery of the Criminal Justice Strategic Plan must be locally led and supported nationally through the following targets and measures.

Effective in bringing offences to justice

By 2011 we will improve the effectiveness and efficiency of the Criminal Justice System in bringing offences to justice, especially serious offences; and the enforcement of the orders of the court including doubling the amount of assets from crime that we recover.

Focus of action for LCJBs

LCJBs will produce plans setting out how they will support delivery of the Crime Strategy, particularly in relation to specific serious offences and locally-identified priorities. They will support offender management, including working with prolific offenders to reduce the risk of re-offending. Through this we will build a more consistent and locally-driven approach focusing LCJBs and local authority partnerships on the priority needs of their areas.

Nationally driven programmes

National measures to tackle serious offences and prolific offending and support regional and local partnerships to tackle crime and reduce re-offending and raise public confidence include:

- new violent crime action plan, including: measures to tackle the specific problem of **violent gangs** in some areas; and robust management of the most dangerous offenders through the Multi-Agency Public Protection Arrangements (MAPPA);
- new performance measures to improve **rape investigation and prosecution,** supported by national training, specialist police and prosecutors and more support for **victims of sexual violence;**
- more effective measures to address **youth offending;**
- **problem solving courts** on topics such as domestic violence and on drugs;
- aligning our approach to persistent young offenders to the **Prolific and other Priority Offender** (PPO) programme;
- joint working with Department of Health to tackle **mental health** issues;
- partnership approach to **reducing re-offending and reintegrating ex-offenders;**
- a co-ordinated approach to the **enforcement of the orders of the court;**
- a robust **asset recovery system** taking the profit out of crime; and
- a new national **anti-fraud strategy.**

The public confident and engaged

By 2011 we will improve public confidence in the fairness and effectiveness of the Criminal Justice System. We will also identify and address race disproportionality at key stages in the criminal justice process. This target will be supported by local indicators for LCJBs on confidence and community engagement.

Focus of action for LCJBs

LCJBs will work with local authority partnerships – Crime and Disorder Reduction Partnerships (CDRPs) and, in Wales, Community Safety Partnerships (CSPs) – to support the Crime Strategy's aim of reducing crime, re-offending and anti-social behaviour. We will ensure a single, integrated process of community consultation and feedback shared between LCJBs and CDRPs/CSPs through common surveys; shared local targets and an integrated planning process.

LCJBs will be asked to develop plans to tackle race disproportionality. We are providing more robust and accurate data, enabling CJS agencies and LCJBs to assess progress and respond to local needs, including indicators to monitor the proportions of people from different ethnic groups at key stages of the CJS. This will enable LCJBs to identify areas of disproportionality and explore why it may be occurring and take appropriate action.

Nationally driven programmes

We will support LCJBs through an overarching Criminal Justice Community Engagement Strategy bringing together the programmes of each criminal justice agency:

- national rollout of **neighbourhood policing** to raise confidence by tackling crime and anti-social behaviour. This will be supported with closer joint working between police and youth justice services. A Neighbourhood Policing Youth Toolkit is currently being assessed;
- prosecution led **community involvement panels;**
- national rollout of **community justice** approach developed in Liverpool and Salford;

- the **breakthrough programme:** measures to improve performance and accountability of the courts; and
- encouraging engagement through **community payback** and **local alliances** to drive down re-offending.

This will be supported by communications programmes including **national campaigns,** the **Justice Awards** and the **Confidence Challenge Fund** and specific measures to reach out to all, particularly ethnic minorities and **tackle hate crime.**

The needs of victims at its heart

By 2011 we will improve victim satisfaction with the police and victim and witness satisfaction with the Criminal Justice System.

Focus of action for LCJBs

We have set standards of service for victims and witnesses through the Victims' Code, Witness Charter and Prosecutor's Pledge and established Witness Care Units providing a single point of contact for support. From November 2006, all police forces have been required to meet service standards set out in the Quality of Service Commitment. This includes improving ease of contact with the police, keeping victims informed of progress and engaging with communities. We will drive delivery of these standards and services to victims through the Victim and Witness Experience Survey (WAVES) giving LCJBs detailed local performance data on how satisfied victims and witnesses are with all aspects of the Criminal Justice System. We will look to improve how victims make their voice heard at local level.

Nationally driven programmes

The following measures will support LCJBs to meet the needs of all victims and witnesses and give victims a voice in the system:

- through the **Victims' Advocate Scheme** and the Crown Prosecution Service **Victim Focus Scheme** we will strengthen measures to **give victims a voice** in the Criminal Justice System;
- we will continue to enhance services to **vulnerable or intimidated witnesses** and those with special needs, especially **victims of the most serious crimes;**

- we will strengthen links between the **voluntary sector** and the Criminal Justice System and divert money from offenders to voluntary sector services through the **Victims' Surcharge;**
- we will make the **Criminal Injuries Compensation Scheme** more customer-focused and continue to develop opportunities for offenders to make amends and pay reparation to their victims and communities.

Simple, efficient processes

By 2011 we will improve the efficiency of the Criminal Justice System in bringing offences to justice; supported with a target to reduce police bureaucracy in response to the Flanagan review of policing.

Focus of action for LCJBs

We will develop simpler, more efficient criminal justice processes by giving LCJBs the tools, targets, flexibility and support needed to develop local programmes of continuous improvement. Through the Beacon Approach we will empower LCJBs to be the key drivers of cross-cutting criminal justice reform, supported nationally by the National Criminal

Justice Board (NCJB). Beacon LCJBs are developing a co-ordinated approach to current change programmes such as the Criminal Justice Simple, Speedy Summary reforms (CJSSS), Conditional Cautions and simplifying case file preparation. Through this approach we will streamline criminal justice processes and reduce police bureaucracy.

Nationally driven programmes

Current national programmes which will be incorporated into this co-ordinated programme of LCJB-led reform include:

- **technology improvements** to free up police time such as hand held computers enabling officers to log crimes on the spot rather than fill in forms;
- **postal charging** to reduce the administration of lower risk cases;
- streamlined **case file preparation** for magistrates' court cases including looking at issues such as disclosure and advance information;
- national rollout of the **CJSSS** reforms to

reduce delay and unnecessary adjournments at court and introduction of a similar programme in the youth court;
- **a legal aid reform** programme to focus on performance and outputs and reduce delay;
- technology to modernise criminal justice processes such as **video links** and a programme to facilitate **electronic preparation and presentation of evidence;** and
- measures to handle low risk, uncontested cases out of court such as **Penalty Notices for Disorder** and the **Conditional Caution.**

National framework, local delivery

National framework, local delivery

Building on the national framework provided by our criminal justice targets and this plan, LCJBs will develop local plans setting out how they will deliver these targets and support delivery of the wider Crime Strategy.

Focus of action for LCJBs

Local boards will work increasingly closely with CDRPs and, in Wales, CSPs to understand the needs and priorities of their area, drawing up plans to deliver criminal justice services aligned to local needs, supported with improved performance data and capacity planning tools provided by the Office for Criminal Justice Reform (OCJR).

Nationally driven programmes

NCJB will work closely with the new National Crime Reduction Board (NCRB) and the National Policing Board (NPB) to coordinate the crime, criminal justice and reducing re-offending strategies. These arrangements are supported by specific groups led at ministerial level, including reducing re-offending. Together these boards will co-ordinate the work of government departments to deliver the wider crime and community safety targets, review overall progress and agree action to address risks to delivery.

NCJB sets the high level vision and targets for the Criminal Justice System with LCJBs increasingly responsible for designing and delivering the programme needed to realise that vision. We will continue to drive forward some national programmes, notably in technology to support criminal justice reform, and setting and monitoring national standards for systems and services. However increasingly we will work by providing the broad principles, including guidance and best practice examples, within which areas develop their approach to meet local circumstances and priorities. We will encourage innovation and feedback from local areas to identify best practice.

1 INTRODUCTION – OUR VISION FOR 2011

1.1 The CJS Strategic Plan for 2011

This Plan sets out how the agencies of the Criminal Justice System (CJS) – the police, prosecution, courts, probation, prison and youth justice services in England and Wales – will work together to reduce crime and re-offending, bring offenders to justice and meet the needs of victims. It sets out our vision and targets for 2011 and how we will develop the partnership between the National Criminal Justice Board (NCJB) and Local Criminal Justice Boards (LCJBs). It is therefore addressed primarily to LCJBs which bring together the chief officers of each of the criminal justice agencies. It is also of interest to others who work in the Criminal Justice System – particularly the judiciary, defence community and voluntary groups such as Victim Support – as well as in Crime and Disorder Reduction and Community Safety Partnerships (CDRPs and CSPs) and the wider public.

1.2 Our vision for the CJS

1.2.1 Our vision is for a Criminal Justice System which puts victims at its heart and in which the public are confident and engaged. It will be effective in bringing offences to justice through simple and efficient processes. In everything we do we will be guided by the following principles:

» **'Effective in bringing offences to justice'** – a system that is effective in bringing crime to justice, especially the most serious, so that it plays its part in reducing crime and re-offending.

» **'The public confident and engaged'** – people in local communities informed about the performance of the system, consulted and engaged about their priorities so they can be confident that it is fair, effective and meets local needs.
» **'The needs of victims at the heart of the system'** – high standards of service for victims and witnesses with the needs of victims at the heart of the system.
» **'Simple, efficient processes'** – speedy, streamlined and efficient processes supported by modern technology that enable the police to focus their time on tackling crime.

1.2.2 To achieve this, criminal justice agencies will work together more closely through LCJBs as well as more effectively with other local partnerships. Whilst we will set a clear national framework and direction, local boards will have more freedom to tailor their priorities and the way they work to address local concerns and needs.

1.2.3 The central purpose of the Criminal Justice System is to deliver an efficient, effective, accountable and fair justice process for the public. By working in partnership with others – illustrated below – it also contributes to wider objectives to cut crime, reduce re-offending and so build safer communities.

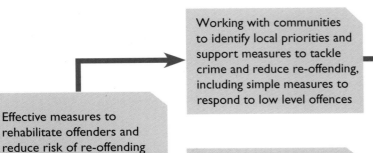

1.3 The story so far – delivery of the 2004-08 Strategic Plan

In July 2004, we published our Strategic Plan for 2004-08. We committed to improve public confidence, increase victim and witness satisfaction, bring more offences to justice through modern and efficient processes and to enforce compliance with sentences and court orders rigorously. By working together, staff from across the system have met – or are on course to meet – almost all of these commitments. This table summarises their achievements[1].

[1]More details are in the following chapters and Annex A.

Commitment - by 2008	Progress to date
The public will have confidence that the CJS is effective and serves all communities fairly.	Public confidence has risen since March 2003 and we have reduced the number of people in ethnic minorities who believe the CJS would treat them worse than other people.
Victims and witnesses will receive a consistent, high standard of service from all CJS agencies.	We have set new standards of service for victims and witnesses.
We will bring more offences to justice.	We brought over 1.4 million offences to justice in the year to June 2007, an increase of 43% since March 2002, and well ahead of target.
We will rigorously enforce the orders of the court.	We have increased the payment rate of fines to 93%, ahead of our target, and met our target of recovering £125 million criminal assets in the year to March 2007.
A joined-up, modern, well run CJS.	We have established the NCJB and LCJBs to drive improved performance across the CJS.

1.4 What still needs to be done – the challenges

1.4.1 We recognise that challenges remain. Crime is down but the rate of reduction has slowed and meeting fully the tough crime reduction target is still a challenge. There is more to do to drive up public confidence, tackle unfair disproportionality and improve the experience of victims and witnesses. We must respond to rising public expectations and the needs of a more mobile and diverse society.

1.4.2 Our performance in bringing offences to justice has improved consistently over the last five years. We now need to focus even harder on more serious crime as well as local priorities whilst recognising the demands that tackling terrorism effectively will place on the system. To do all this, we need to improve the efficiency of our processes and our use of resources.

1.4.3 There is more to do to ensure that minor offences and anti-social behaviour by young people can be effectively dealt with by local children's services and voluntary sector preventive programmes. We need to drive up awareness and confidence in the youth justice system, highlighting the achievements that have taken place since the youth justice reforms of 1998. At the same time we must find new ways to respond to growing public concerns about guns, gangs and knives.

1.4.4 Although we have delivered the basic IT infrastructure and many of the case management systems for joining up the Criminal Justice System, technology on its own will not deliver a joined-up service. Staff tell us that the Criminal Justice System is too complex and that we can do more to streamline our processes and drive a more co-ordinated approach to reform.

NEW PSA FRAMEWORK

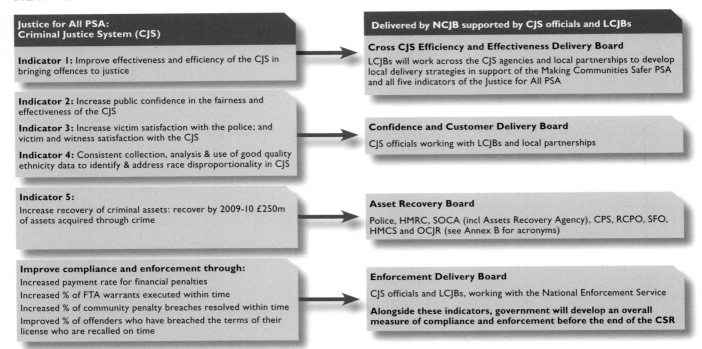

1.5 What we aim to deliver: our targets

1.5.1 As part of the 2007 Comprehensive Spending Review, we have launched new targets for the period 2008-11 set out in our Public Service Agreements (PSAs). These provide the framework for addressing the challenges. The crime and criminal justice targets have been developed jointly and bring together two key aims: reducing crime and re-offending through the *Making Communities Safer* PSA target and delivering justice through the criminal justice PSA target. The criminal justice PSA target *Justice for All* supports the Crime Strategy and the *Making Communities Safer* PSA by focusing on increasing the effectiveness and efficiency of the CJS in bringing offences to justice, especially serious offences[2].

1.5.2 The Criminal Justice Strategic Plan also supports and contributes to a number of cross government targets, which are set out in the diagram overleaf.

1.5.3 Delivery of these targets requires closer working between national criminal justice agencies and local authority services. The new performance framework and Local Area Agreements (LAAs) provide local authorities and partners with the flexibility to deliver the best solutions for their areas through a new relationship with central Government, giving greater flexibility to respond to their communities' needs. LCJBs will support this new approach by working more closely with local partnerships.

The PSA targets, where they relate to devolved matters, do not apply to Wales. However, the Criminal Justice System in Wales pursues the same targets as in England and works in partnership with the Welsh Assembly Government to develop joint ownership of other cross-departmental outcome measures. For example, the Welsh Assembly Government has adopted targets to reduce first time entrants to the youth justice system under the *All Wales Youth Offending Strategy*, and increase the number of young offenders in education, training and employment as one of the outcome measures for *Children and Youth People's Plans* in each local authority in Wales.

[2] As with all government PSA targets, they are supported with a delivery agreement which sets out how the target will be delivered and measured and which is published on the HM Treasury website. (See Annex C for references)

CJS CONTRIBUTION TO OTHER PUBLIC SERVICES AGREEMENTS

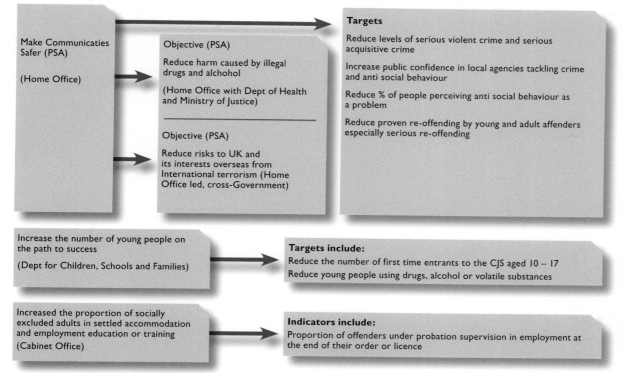

Make Communicaties Safer (PSA)

(Home Office)

Objective (PSA)

Reduce harm caused by illegal drugs and alchohol

(Home Office with Dept of Health and Ministry of Justice)

Objective (PSA)

Reduce risks to UK and its interests overseas from International terrorism (Home Office led, cross-Government)

Targets

Reduce levels of serious violent crime and serious acquisitive crime

Increase public confidence in local agencies tackling crime and anti social behaviour

Reduce % of people perceiving anti social behaviour as a problem

Reduce proven re-offending by young and adult affenders especially serious re-offending

Increase the number of young people on the path to success

(Dept for Children, Schools and Families)

Targets include:
Reduce the number of first time entrants to the CJS aged 10 – 17
Reduce young people using drugs, alcohol or volatile substances

Increased the proportion of socially excluded adults in settled accommodation and employment education or training
(Cabinet Office)

Indicators include:
Proportion of offenders under probation supervision in employment at the end of their order or licence

1.6 How we aim to deliver: a new partnership between the NCJB and LCJBs

1.6.1 We are setting a new direction in the partnership between the NCJB and local boards. LCJBs have achieved a great deal and together met most of the national performance targets. Following pilot work in Greater Manchester and Devon and Cornwall, it is clear that given the right support and greater freedom, they can make a real impact on the efficiency and effectiveness of the service they provide. We are building on this through a 'Beacon Approach' being developed in ten local areas. The Beacon Approach means that whilst Ministers and the NCJB, in consultation with LCJBs, set the strategic direction and outcomes for the system, LCJBs will increasingly be given far greater freedom over the definition and implementation of 'how' this will be done.

1.6.2 This is therefore a different kind of strategic planning document. Instead of a prescriptive list of changes delivered in the same way by all boards, this plan sets out a clear vision for reform but gives LCJBs the flexibility to tailor service improvement to local needs and priorities, locally driving innovation. The NCJB will continue to challenge and support local boards to achieve high levels of service and greater efficiency. But increasingly that challenge will come not over the detail of individual performance targets or changes but over the quality of outcomes and efficiency of the services provided.

Developing the Partnership Approach – working with Crime and Disorder Reduction Partnerships/Community Safety Partnerships

1.6.3 At the same time, LCJBs will also increasingly work closely with CDRPs and, in Wales, CSPs. This requires joint work on engaging communities to understand local priorities to drive their shared responsibility to build safer communities.

The framework of this strategic plan

1.6.4 In each of the chapters that follow we set out:

» **The vision and targets** for 2011 – the PSA targets: those led by the Criminal Justice System and LCJBs and those to which LCJBs make a supporting contribution.

» **The focus of action for LCJBs** – key areas of action for local boards in delivering or supporting delivery of these targets.

» **The planning framework for local delivery** – the way local boards and CDRPs/CSPs will work together to integrate local planning.

» The context of **nationally driven programmes and initiatives** – these may be promising pilot projects or programmes which have been tested and are being rolled out across the country. In the future these will increasingly comprise initiatives begun in local areas and local boards will have greater freedom to select initiatives which meet their requirements.

1.7 What will be different

The public's concerns are not with how we work together but the outcomes delivered. But we believe that by giving local boards greater freedom and responsibility to improve the service they provide, we will make further substantial improvements to the quality of service experienced by the public. This will mean:

For victims and witnesses: more confidence to come forward, expecting and receiving a high, tailored level of service from reporting the crime through to sentence and beyond with special measures for the vulnerable. Information on the progress of cases and support services to help set right – as far as possible – the consequences of the crime.

For communities and the law-abiding majority: people from all communities will have greater understanding of and confidence in the fairness and effectiveness of the system, particularly their local Criminal Justice System. They will have the opportunity to influence criminal justice priorities in their area and contribute to their delivery knowing that the system is becoming more effective in tackling local priorities and more serious offending.

For all users of the Criminal Justice System: whether victims, witnesses, jurors, defendants or offenders a more efficient, fair and effective system which builds confidence: a system increasingly able to identify and address any unfair disproportionality.

For members of staff, criminal justice practitioners and volunteers: the information needed to speak with more confidence about the justice system as a whole, not just individual organisations, and to engage with the local community. More opportunities for joint working and interchange, to achieve better outcomes for the public, whilst respecting professional boundaries and independence.

2 EFFECTIVE IN BRINGING OFFENCES TO JUSTICE

Effective in bringing offences to justice
– a system that is effective in bringing crime to justice so that the Criminal Justice System plays its part in reducing crime and re-offending.

2.1 Why this matters

2.1.1 The fundamental test of any justice system is its effectiveness in bringing offences to justice. This means that the prosecution process is well managed, the guilty convicted and the innocent acquitted in a way that meets the needs of victims and treats all sections of the community fairly. We have had a major focus over the last few years on tackling cases that failed simply because they were not ready or because witnesses were not called or prepared to give evidence.

2.1.2 Effectiveness is more than this. It means engaging with communities and responding to local priorities. It means criminal justice helping to deter crime because offenders know that they will be caught and punished and ensuring that when caught, they do not re-offend. This is about taking account of both offence and offender. It is about public protection and harm reduction – focussing resources on the most serious offences and persistent offenders, with custody for those who present a danger to the public, and effective, challenging community penalties others. It is about tough enforcement and taking the profit out of crime through recovery of criminal assets. The public needs confidence that offenders are being punished and that crime does not pay. But they also want to know that offenders are effectively rehabilitated back into society.

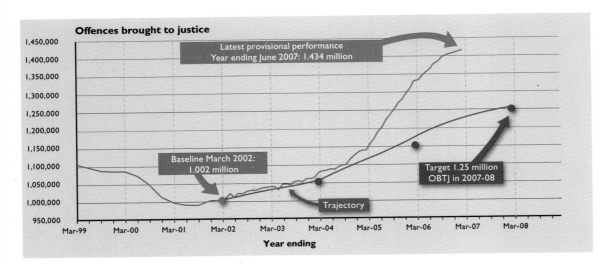

2.1.3 Although many agencies beyond the Criminal Justice System have a part to play in this, this chapter sets out the role of the Criminal Justice System itself and in particular LCJBs.

2.2 The story so far

2.2.1 We have made progress in all of these areas. Crime and re-offending are down. We have brought more offences to justice, improved witness attendance at court and delivered major improvements in the effectiveness of trials.

2.2.2 Through the provision of effective measures such as the Prolific and other Priority Programme (PPO) and Drug Interventions Programme (DIP), targeting the most persistent offenders, we have successfully reduced re-offending. The latest statistics on adult re-offending in England and

Wales show a reduction of 5.8% when comparing 2004 to 2000[3]. Since the introduction of the DIP, recorded acquisitive crime has fallen by 20%[4] and over 3,000 offenders a month enter drug treatment.

2.2.3 We have strengthened all parts of the system to ensure an effective response to all types of crime. For example the Serious Organised Crime Agency (SOCA) began operations in April 2006 – bringing together police, customs and immigration experts to tackle serious crimes including human trafficking, major fraud and drugs trafficking and recovering related criminal assets. We have also delivered considerable improvements in enforcing the orders of the court, particularly in the recovery of fines and assets from offenders. We have changed the law so that criminals must prove that they have obtained their money through legitimate means.

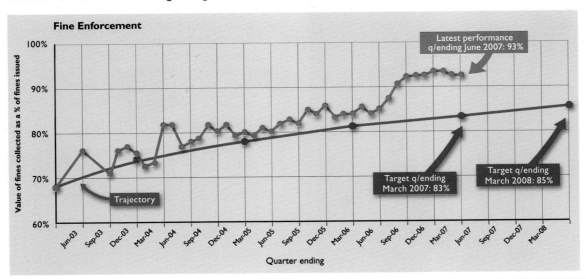

[3] Re-offending of adults: results from the 2004 cohort" available at http://www.homeoffice.gov.uk/rds/pdfs07/hosb0607.pdf.
[4] From 3.7 million recorded offences in 2002/03 to 2.9 million in 2006/07.

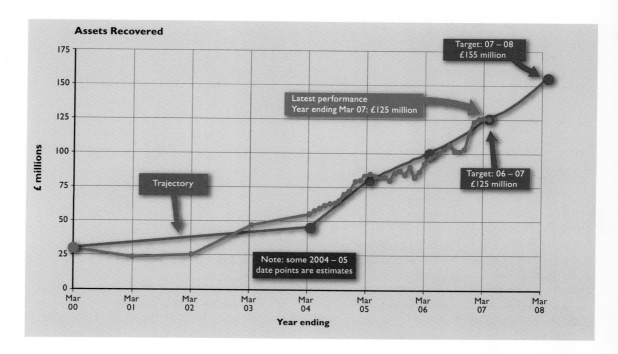

Assets Recovered

Target: 07 – 08
£155 million

Latest performance
Year ending Mar 07: £125 million

Trajectory

Target: 06 – 07
£125 million

Note: some 2004 – 05
date points are estimates

£ millions

Year ending

2.3 Our vision and targets for 2011

2.3.1 **Our vision is for a system that is more effective in bringing crime to justice so that the Criminal Justice System plays its part in reducing crime and re-offending.** To achieve this a greater focus is needed on the most serious offences and persistent offenders. LCJBs need to respond more visibly to local priorities, including effective responses to anti-social behaviour. We must raise the profile of effective community interventions, enforce them firmly and communicate their success building public confidence in them.

2.3.2 We need to ensure that the sentences and orders of the court are robustly enforced and opportunities for recovering criminal assets are widened, so that offenders see that they will be held to account and that crime does not pay.

CJS / LCJB targets to support delivery of our vision for a Criminal Justice System which is more effective in bringing offences to justice

Justice for All PSA 1: improve the effectiveness and efficiency of the CJS in bringing offences to justice
Justice for All PSA 5: increase recovery of criminal assets
Justice for All: supporting indicator – improve compliance and enforcement

The CJS and LCJBs also support Safer Communities PSA targets on:
reducing levels of serious violent crime and serious acquisitive crime
reducing proven re-offending

2.4 Focus of Action for LCJBs

We have worked with LCJBs to define more clearly their role in bringing offences to justice in a way which supports work to reduce crime and re-offending. The focus of action for LCJBs should be:

» **Violent and sexual offences:** improving performance not just in terms of the number of offences brought to justice but also in dealing more effectively with more serious sexual or violent offences such as rape.

» **Building confidence and responding to local priorities:** helping to reduce the fear of crime by making the system visibly and effectively respond to local priorities as set out in chapter three.

» **Tackling the problems underlying offending behaviour:** providing more opportunities during the prosecution process to focus on how to tackle the underlying needs of offenders, especially those which relate to their offending behaviour, tailoring the response to crime to the offence and the offender.

» **Effective enforcement:** ensuring that once sentences are imposed, they are rigorously enforced and monitored with a stronger emphasis on first time compliance.

» **Taking the profit out of crime:** sending a clear message that crime does not pay, by ensuring that we recover criminal assets.

2.5 The Partnership and Planning Framework for Local Delivery

2.5.1 LCJBs will draw up a local delivery plan based on an analysis of crime in their area showing how they will do more to tackle all aspects of crime, especially more serious crime and local priorities. To do this, LCJBs will need to work with CDRPs/CSPs to consider:

» the evidence from tools such as the National Intelligence Model about the reality of crime in their area;

» the results of consultation with local communities about priorities and concerns about crime;

» the performance of the Criminal Justice System in bringing different types of crime to justice and in particular, the most serious crimes; and

» the most effective ways of dealing with the offence and offender types that emerge from this assessment of demand.

2.5.2 In some areas, integrated delivery planning between LCJBs and CDRPs/ CSPs already occurs but in others it does not. We will therefore be supporting all areas to begin to work in this way for 2008-09.

2.5.3 We will continue to drive improvements in the enforcement of the orders of the court, agreeing precise targets through the annual business planning process. We will continue to focus on:

» community penalty breach – reducing the time from breach to effective resolution;

» licence recall – getting offenders who breach back into custody;

» fine payment; and

» failure to attend warrants – ensuring defendants turn up for court hearings.

2.5.4 We will increase our focus on ensuring first time compliance and will develop a programme and set of measures to support LCJBs in this.

2.5.5 Our new target for asset recovery is to double current performance and seize £250 million a year by 2009-10 with the longer term aim of detecting up to £1 billion. We will agree local targets to support this aim. We will also increase the proportion of cases in which the proceeds of crime are pursued and improve our cooperation in chasing assets internationally, increasing the risk of loss to drug traffickers and other serious criminals operating in the UK.

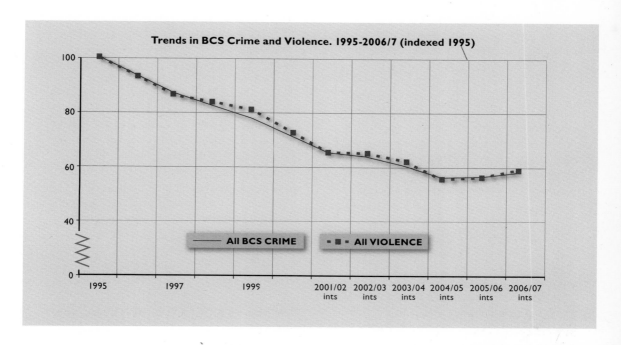

Trends in BCS Crime and Violence. 1995-2006/7 (indexed 1995)

2.6 Nationally Driven Programmes and Initiatives

2.6.1 In drawing up their plans, LCJBs will need to be aware of the nationally driven programmes and initiatives that set the context for their work and from which they are able to draw to support local delivery. Although not a comprehensive list, the programmes and initiatives most relevant to bringing offences to justice more effectively are set out on the following pages. They contribute to the Government's wider crime agenda summarised overleaf.

Tackling violent crime

2.6.2 Although overall violent crime, as measured by BCS, has decreased by 31% since 1997 (see above), there is more to do to tackle certain types of violent crime, improve performance in some areas and support victims. We will be publishing a violent crime action plan later in 2007.

Tackling sexual violence and rape and supporting victims

2.6.3 A range of actions to improve the investigation and prosecution of rape was set out in the cross-government *Action Plan on Sexual Violence and Abuse* published in April 2007. A new set of performance measures to monitor

rape investigation and prosecution has been established. Specialist officers and specialist rape prosecutors are now operating across most of England and Wales and national training programmes are being rolled out. All police force areas have developed an action plan to be delivered in partnership with the CPS and other agencies. LCJBs will be asked to look particularly at their performance in bringing offences of rape to justice.

2.6.4 As part of this we need to give victims the confidence they will be supported if they come forward. We are extending the network of Sexual Assault Referral Centres: there are currently 19 and it is our ambition that there will be 36 by the end of 2007-08. We are piloting and evaluating the role of Independent Sexual Violence Advisors based in voluntary sector organisations, providing advocacy and support for victims in 38 areas in England and Wales. Through the Victims Fund we also provide funding for voluntary organisations to support victims of sexual violence.

Domestic violence

2.6.5 Tackling domestic violence is a priority across government. It is driven forward through the Domestic Violence National Delivery Plan, co-ordinated by the Home Office. Multi Agency Risk Assessment Conferences (MARACs) now meet in many areas to respond to victims

The Crime Strategy: Cutting Crime – a New Partnership 2008, published in July 2007, sets out the Government's approach to preventing and tackling crime. It outlines the need to continue pressure on reducing anti-social behaviour and serious acquisitive crime, a stronger focus on tackling more serious violence, and a drive to increase public confidence in local agencies. Early intervention, prevention, enforcement and reducing re-offending are key elements of our approach to tackling crime, along with continued pressure on the cross-cutting drivers of crime such as drug and alcohol misuse, and social exclusion.

The objectives in the Criminal Justice Strategic Plan align closely with the delivery of the crime strategy. An efficient and effective Criminal Justice System, robust in dealing with serious crime in particular, is a crucial factor in delivering reductions in crime and anti-social behaviour and increasing public confidence, deterring future crime and ensuring appropriate sanctions for crime committed. Similarly, the Crime Strategy emphasises the need to focus on the offender as well as the offence – dealing with offenders appropriately in terms of enforcement, but also working to reduce their reoffending. The Criminal Justice Strategic Plan, and forthcoming Reducing Re-offending Strategic Plan, both represent key drivers in the wider delivery of the Crime Strategy.

The Crime Strategy outlines the need for a greater focus on more serious violence (including sexual offending) and reducing the harm it causes. This is reflected in the new *Making Communities Safer* PSA 2008-09/ 2010-11, setting a specific measure for tackling violent crime and sexual offending. This should drive a stronger focus on serious violence, not just by CDRPs/ CSPs but throughout the Criminal Justice System, building on innovative and successful work such as Domestic Violence Courts. More detail on action to tackle specific elements of violent crime and sexual offending will be published by the end of 2007.

Increasing public confidence, in particular through greater engagement of communities, is a key aim of the Crime Strategy. It underpins a desired new relationship between Government and delivery partners, where Government will focus more strongly on outcomes and adding value in areas such as design against crime, and local partners have greater flexibility to respond to local priorities (and focus more on engaging local communities in order to understand local priorities sufficiently). LCJBs and CDRPs/CSPs need to work closely on their plans for engaging local communities and understanding local priorities, to ensure engagement between local partners and communities is coherent, does not duplicate, and feeds into a shared sense of local priorities right across the CJS and wider crime reduction partners.

The delivery of the Crime Strategy is co-ordinated at national level through the National Crime Reduction Board (NCRB). This board has a close relationship with the National Criminal Justice Board (NCJB), ensuring there is strong continuity and national co-ordination on the delivery of objectives common to both, or mutually complementary. One of the supporting boards of the NCRB and NCJB is the Reducing Re-offending Inter-Ministerial Group, overseeing delivery of the reducing reoffending programme, integral to delivery of the Crime Strategy.

The Ministry of Justice and Department of Innovation, Universities and Skills will be consulting on a new three year cross-government Reducing Re-offending Strategic Plan to be published in spring 2008 which will support the delivery of the new cross government PSAs on Safer Communities, Drugs and Alcohol, and Social Exclusion. The plan will promote national, regional and local partnership working; support the continued delivery of an end-to-end offender management programme; and effective local delivery of the aims of both the Crime and Re-offending Strategies.

of domestic violence to prevent repeat victimisation. This is supported by the Specialist Domestic Violence Court (SDVC) Programme. Evaluation of two pilots in Caerphilly and Croydon demonstrated significant benefits for the courts and victims:

» better information sharing and more effective services and support for victims, leading to improved victim satisfaction and increased confidence in the Criminal Justice System;

» increased number of domestic violence incidents reported that resulted in a case at court, more guilty pleas and convictions; and

» reduced number of cases discontinued and withdrawn before trial.

2.6.6 Courts involved in the programme work strategically with local statutory and voluntary partners and may alter their listing arrangements to cluster and/or fast-track domestic violence cases. Magistrates receive specialist training to understand the context in which domestic violence cases arise. In April 2007, there were 64 SDVCs and we will continue to develop the approach.

Tackling gangs

2.6.7 To address the specific problem of violence by criminal gangs in some areas, we have set up a new dedicated national unit to run a "tackling gangs" action programme. It is overseen by a central ministerial taskforce on guns and gangs, chaired by the Home Secretary. Neighbourhoods in parts of London, Liverpool, Greater Manchester and Birmingham will be the focus of renewed action to tackle gun crime and serious violence among young people. These areas have been identified by the police as suffering disproportionately from problems with criminal gangs which can be involved in gun crime and present the greatest challenges. These hotspots account for over half of all firearms offences in England and Wales

2.6.8 The programme includes a range of measures such as covert operations against targeted gang members; visible police presence on the streets in the gang areas, including on routes to and from schools, safe houses for victims and witnesses and those seeking to leave gangs and greater witness protection. In the

CASE STUDY:

WOMEN'S SAFETY UNIT IN CARDIFF
Jan Pickles, Manager, Cardiff Safety Unit, has revolutionised the way in which victims of domestic violence are supported in Cardiff. She set up and secured funding for a Women's Safety Unit in Cardiff, a local voluntary organisation which has raised awareness of domestic violence in the police, prosecution, the judiciary as well as health and social care agencies. She worked with other key agencies including South Wales Police who have provided a designated officer based in the unit. The results of Jan's efforts have led to an increase in the number of domestic violence cases that proceed to conviction and a big reduction in the level of re-offending in Cardiff. The Cardiff model, adopted as the Home Office's Co-ordinated Community Response to Domestic Violence, is now national policy. The multi-agency risk assessment conferences (MARACs) created in Cardiff have now been rolled out to 60 areas as an example of good multi-agency working. MARACs bring together all the agencies involved – health, education, social care and the voluntary sector as well as criminal justice agencies to identify high risk cases, share information and agree action plans to reduce the risk of domestic violence to victims and their children. Evaluation has indicated that this approach has been very effective: over 42% of victims at risk of domestic homicide are safe at the follow-up point after a year. Others ask for help earlier, having confidence the system can help them and their children. This means no more suffering in silence. Jan's contribution to supporting victims of domestic violence led to her receiving a Justice Award in 2004 and an OBE later that year.

longer term the tackling gangs action programme will also work on improving our understanding of serious violence among young people, looking not only at the use of lethal weapons but at youth disorder, anti-social behaviour, neighbourhood renewal and prevention.

Building confidence and responding to local priorities

2.6.9 The joint planning approach LCJBs will be developing with their CDRPs and CSPs will provide the means for more effective engagement with local areas, to understand their priorities and needs. We describe this further in chapters three and six. Existing evidence shows that a key priority for local communities is the need to do more to tackle anti-social behaviour. We will be leading a fresh drive to increase take up of Individual Support Orders (ISOs), Acceptable Behaviour Contracts (ABCs) and other positive interventions provided by Youth Offending Teams (YOTs) helping young people address their behaviour, but with sanctions if they do not. This builds on current prevention programmes such as Youth Inclusion Programmes and the Safer Schools Partnerships. It also builds on the collaborative work undertaken by the criminal justice agencies to raise awareness of the use of ISOs amongst multi-agency local authority teams tackling anti social behaviour.

Young offenders – more effective and joined-up measures

2.6.10 The Crime Strategy announced the development of a cross-government *Youth Crime Action Plan*, to be published in spring 2008 which will set out the Government's approach to youth crime and justice from early intervention and prevention, through to reducing re-offending.

2.6.11 The Criminal Justice System sits at the centre of our wider strategy on youth crime. To improve its effectiveness, we are developing a sentencing framework for young people that provides robust community-based alternatives to custody. This will include simpler court penalties, such as our proposal in the *Criminal Justice and Immigration Bill* 2006-07 for a Youth Rehabilitation Order (YRO) which will be the new generic community sentence for under-18s. This will clarify the community sentencing structure and form part of a new end-to-end, scaled, risk-based approach to the supervision of children and young people who offend. The YRO will include intensive supervision and surveillance and intensive fostering options recognisable as

In Wales, the principles underlying Welsh Assembly Government Policy on youth justice are contained in the *All Wales Youth Offending Strategy*, published jointly with the Youth Justice Board in 2004. The Strategy provides a national framework for preventing offending and re-offending among children and young people in Wales. An expert group, including public and voluntary agencies in Wales, meets quarterly to take forward implementation of the Strategy by means of a series of annual objectives and targets. The Assembly provides support for implementation of the Strategy through the Safer Communities Fund providing grant funding to the 22 Community Safety Partnerships in Wales.

the last steps before custody and which will be designed for those young offenders who would (if this option did not exist) be subject to a custodial sentence.

2.6.12 As part of our commitment to tackle lower risk youth offending more effectively, the *Criminal Justice and Immigration Bill* includes a provision to extend Conditional Cautions to 16-17 year olds. We are also reviewing the role of Attendance Centres to build them into our overall approach to tackling lower risk youth offending.

2.6.13 We are considering a youth restorative justice disposal enabling police patrols to remain on the beat whilst using restorative justice to handle first, minor offences by young people through an on-the-spot apology and agreed resolution. This would divert the most minor offences from the formal justice system. Restorative justice is a key principle of the youth justice system. It brings victims, offenders and communities together to decide on a response to a particular crime. It puts victims' needs at the heart of the Criminal Justice System, finding positive solutions to crime and encouraging offenders to face up to and take responsibility for their actions. Research published by the Ministry of Justice in 2007[5] found 85% of victims and 80% of offenders were satisfied with their experience of a Restorative Justice conference.

[5]Shapland et al, 2007.

Neighbourhood policing youth toolkit

2.6.14 The Association of Chief Police Officers (ACPO) and the Youth Justice Board (YJB) have developed a Neighbourhood Policing Youth Toolkit to improve the combined police/youth offending team (YOT) response to crime by focusing more strongly on:

» detection and intelligence gathering;
» embedding a common risk assessment approach; and
» timely and effective interventions to reduce anti social behaviour, crime and re-offending, in partnership with mainstream services such as health.

2.6.15 The toolkit will use a staged approach aiming to divert the most minor offences out of the formal Criminal Justice System through problem solving and restorative approaches and focusing resources on those most at risk of re-offending. It will help police and YOTs to focus on high risk individuals and their families and enable better preventative and crime reduction work. The toolkit will be piloted in three police basic command unit (BCU) areas in the Metropolitan Police and Essex.

Reducing re-offending – problem solving approaches and specialist expertise

2.6.16 The Criminal Justice System can make a real contribution to reducing re-offending by helping offenders during the prosecution process to address underlying problems linked to offending. This means ensuring that there are appropriate links to specialist assessment and referral services and that sentencers have high quality support and information about these services. Specialist expertise and problem-solving courts can help achieve this. They aim to address the specific causes and consequences of particular types of crime and reduce re-offending. They also encourage the engagement of victims in the process. The work may be clustered in specialist lists but may equally be mainstreamed in regular court business.

2.6.17 Currently models have been developed to target anti-social behaviour, domestic violence and low level acquisitive crime driven by Class A drug misuse. Pilot drug courts at Leeds and West

London magistrates' courts were launched in December 2005. Independent evaluation will be completed in 2007 to inform decisions on further roll-out of this model.

2.6.18 Through the Community Justice pilot initiatives, described in chapter three, we will monitor and evaluate the use of Section 178 provisions in the *Criminal Justice Act 2003* which enable the judge to call offenders back to review the progress of the completion of their Community Order and refer them on to other services where appropriate. We will focus this provision on those most at risk of re-offending. Closer monitoring of the offender and the increased support available will increase compliance with community orders, prevent re-offending and increase the public's confidence in community orders.

2.6.19 These models provide a flexible approach that can be tailored and operated in a court centre to meet local priorities and needs. For example, West London Magistrates' Court has both a Dedicated Drug Court and a Specialist Domestic Violence Court system.

Mental health

2.6.20. There is a much higher prevalence of mental disorder among offenders than within the general population. We want to ensure that there are more effective arrangements for assessment and referral during the prosecution process but also ensure that the prosecution can proceed if that is appropriate. To do this, we are developing stronger joint structures and an agreed good practice approach between the Criminal Justice System and NHS. The *National Offender Health and Social Care Strategy* (to be published in spring 2008) will support the delivery of health and social care services in line with NHS and Social Care Standards, for people at any point in the Criminal Justice System. The strategy will promote better access at all points in the criminal justice process, to evidence-based, effective, mental health services including early intervention, assessment, treatment and ongoing support.

2.6.21 We are also piloting in England an audit "checklist" to help local Criminal Justice System agencies and mental health services develop good practice in dealing with mentally disordered offenders, and to allow for an objective measure of the cost-effectiveness of good practice. Building on this, we will develop protocols to help Criminal Justice System and health professionals determine how to work together to build the capacity of services to respond to need. In Wales, the Welsh Assembly Government is tracking the developments outlined above and will be seeking appropriate improvements

A joined-up approach to tackling prolific and priority offenders

2.6.22 The DIP and PPO programmes are now aligned, enabling us to improve the management of all prolific and priority offenders, including those drugs misusers causing the most harm. The PPO programme is a comprehensive, staged approach, with three strands:

» **prevent and deter:** intensive work with young offenders on the cusp of becoming prolific offenders;

» **catch and convict:** a managed, multi-agency approach to tackle the offending behaviour of those committing most crime and causing most harm to their communities; and

» **rehabilitate and resettle:** multi-agency work providing supportive interventions to help offenders tackle the underlying behaviour related to their offending and reduce the risk of re-offending. PPOs are offered the opportunity for rehabilitation but if they re-offend, they face a swift return to the courts.

2.6.23 As part of their joint planning with CDRPs/CSPs, LCJBs will look at how to direct their resources towards managing those offenders who present the highest risk of harm and offend the most. LCJBs have a key role in driving a joined up approach to prolific offenders. Offender managers will focus their time on those who pose the most serious risk of harm and the most prolific offenders, using the PPO programme to ensure quick listing of cases and prompt breach action for non compliance. LCJBs have responsibility for driving the PPO CJS Premium Service and ensuring there is more robust management of key priority cases, including those offenders being managed by local PPO schemes. The PPO Prevent and Deter Strand will be augmented to give additional focus on prevention

and the supporting role of Children's Services: this approach will be highlighted in the Neighbourhood Policing Youth Toolkit being jointly developed by ACPO and the YJB.

2.6.24 Although the Persistent Young Offender (PYO) pledge remains at 71 days for 2007/08 the NCJB introduced a 65 day stretch target for LCJBs from January 2007 for the Pledge. This was supported by a more robust performance management regime, to ensure all agencies continued to scrutinise their policies and standards. Building on the success of this focus we are developing work to bring the PYO and PPO approaches together with more outcome-focussed targets, including both timeliness and re-offending. The new PSA targets provide an opportunity to streamline our approach making best use of resources and focussing on harm reduction, public protection and effectiveness as well as timeliness. We set out in chapter six how joint working between LCJBs and local partnerships will support this approach.

CASE STUDY:

THE PIER PROJECT IN MERSEYSIDE
The Pier Project in Merseyside is a multi-agency team including police and probation officers, who are responsible for monitoring and supervising members of the community who have been identified as Prolific and other Priority Offenders (PPOs). These are usually chaotic drug users who commit crime to fund drug addictions. If an offender on the PPO list does re-offend, they are targeted and swiftly dealt with through the CJS. However the Pier Project also provides support to help them stop offending. Members of the team assist offenders in gaining basic skills, help arrange accommodation and, as they reform and stop offending, provide training for job interviews. The project has led to a significant reduction in the types of acquisitive crime which these offenders commit. In the Wirral area, burglary fell from 217 offences in February 2004 to 93 in February 2006 and vehicle crime fell from 201 to 89 offences in the same period. The project team won a Justice Award in 2006.

More effective and joined up measures to reduce re-offending by reintegrating ex-offenders

2.6.25 Effective support for offenders as they complete their sentence is important to help them re-integrate and not re-offend. The cross-government *National Reducing Re-offending Delivery Plan*, launched in November 2005, outlines the Government's commitment on improving offenders' access to mainstream services across the seven pathways as identified by the Social Exclusion Unit's report on *Reducing Re-offending by ex-Prisoners*:

» Accommodation,
» Skills and employment,
» Children and Families,
» Finance, Benefit and Debt,
» Attitudes, Thinking and Behaviour,
» Drugs and Alcohol
» Tackling Health Inequalities

2.6.26 Strong joint commissioning and partnership working at a national, regional and local level underpins work to re-integrate offenders successfully into communities, reducing the risk of re-offending. Under the commissioning and contestability arrangements, Probation Boards and Trusts will become lead providers for services. Probation trusts will have a key role representing NOMS when working with LCJBs and a range of local partnerships. This work is supported by Reducing Re-offending Alliances with the public, private and voluntary sectors and local communities described in chapter three.

Effective enforcement

2.6.27 Through the National Enforcement Service NES pathfinder initiative in the North West of England we have been testing a more co-ordinated approach to enforcing the orders and sentences of the court. The initiative is aimed at improving the way enforcement professionals work to maximise compliance and deliver a cross-Criminal Justice System enforcement operation that is highly visible, focussed, professional and collaborative. This will enable us to better co-ordinate and reinforce our efforts, particularly against the "hard core" of defaulters. This work will ensure:

» greater efficiency through reduced duplication and improved information and data sharing between agencies; and
» improvements in compliance with the orders of the court, including: the payment rate for fines; a concerted drive to reduce the number of outstanding warrants for offenders failing to appear at court; and, improvements in compliance with community sentences.

CASE STUDY:

U HAVE TEXT!
Following the North West NES pathfinder initiative, the text messaging system has now been successfully rolled out nationally. As a result magistrates' courts across England and Wales have the ability to send text messages to fine evaders demanding they pay up. Feedback received from magistrates' courts across England and Wales indicate that approximately 25,000 text messages were sent by staff to defaulters in the last four months. Due to the high level of usage, the cost of sending a text message by magistrates' courts to a defaulter has been reduced from 8p to 6.8p. A recent evaluation shows that on average £20 in outstanding fines is recouped per text that is sent. This is having a positive effect on the enforcement of court orders. Feedback from staff indicates that the text messaging application is both quick and simple to use.

Taking the profit out of crime

2.6.28 A robust asset recovery system reduces the harm caused by crime and helps take the profit out of crime. We will design systems and tools that identify and respond flexibly to changing trends in disguising and laundering criminal assets. We are developing a partnership approach across agencies with shared targets and governance promoting joint working to maximise effective asset recovery. We are analysing how to improve the effectiveness of the flow of cases through the system, whether through seizure and forfeiture, restraint and confiscation or civil recovery.

CASE STUDY:

MISSING TRADER AND CAROUSEL FRAUD

This is a highly sophisticated EU-wide scam. Criminals import high-value low volume goods such as mobile phones and computer chips, free of VAT, from other countries in the EU. These goods are then sold in the UK with VAT added, but the criminals disappear with the tax they have collected instead of handing it over to HM Revenue and Customs (HMRC), hence the term "missing trader". A more complicated form of the fraud, known as Carousel fraud, involves the same goods being traded within and beyond the EU, re-entering the UK on a number of occasions with VAT being retained by the fraudsters each time. This is not a victimless crime, but organised fraud on a massive scale perpetrated by criminals. This is theft of revenue needed to fund the country's public services. It often includes links to other crimes.

In June 2007, after one of the largest ever investigations by HMRC, involving nearly 100 mobile phone traders, RCPO successfully prosecuted six men who were behind an £85 million VAT "Carousel" fraud. The six men were subsequently jailed for a total of over 47 years. This was an excellent example of an investigation and prosecution team working together effectively in the fight against crime.

It is RCPO's policy to pursue confiscation proceedings in order to strip the guilty of assets illegally derived from the proceeds of these frauds. This aspect of the case is still underway. All those sentenced were also disqualified from directorships of UK registered companies.

2.6.29 To support the enforcement of confiscation orders, HMCS has established nine regional Centres of Excellence. The CPS is continuing its confiscation training programme delivering training to prosecutors across the country on money laundering and enforcement and is looking to extend this to improved

advocacy in confiscation hearings. HM Revenue and Customs Prosecutions Office (RCPO) has established a dedicated Asset Forfeiture Division to prosecute cases from HMRC, co-operating closely with Criminal Justice System colleagues in asset recovery.

Fraud Review

2.6.30 In 2006 the *Government Fraud Review Report* was published. It recommended a government-led national anti-fraud strategy to provide leadership and cross-cutting co-ordination, ensuring anti-fraud efforts are effective and efficient. The Attorney General has been leading work to design plans for implementation of the key recommendations. Dedicated funding is in place for the Attorney General, Home Office and the City of London Police to fund the initial building blocks of the National Fraud Strategy: a National Fraud Strategic Authority, a fraud loss measurement unit, a National Fraud Reporting and Intelligence Centre and a National Lead Force for Fraud. Work progresses on other elements of the implementation plans.

2.6.31 The national strategy will ensure that:

» knowledge of fraud is managed effectively;
» activity across the system is properly co-ordinated for maximum impact;
» law makers and law enforcers work together to radically change the balance of risk and reward against criminals; and
» the system earns public confidence by delivering justice and redress for victims.

2.6.32 For the first time, the UK will have a managed programme that attacks fraud through the entire pipeline of deterrence, prevention, detection, investigation, sanction and redress to victims.

3 ENGAGING COMMUNITIES

The public confident and engaged
– people in local communities informed about the performance of the system, consulted and engaged about their priorities so they can be confident that it is fair, effective and meets local needs.

3.1 Why this matters

3.1.1 The Criminal Justice System belongs to the people it serves. An effective justice system which people trust to protect them, do justice, and reflect their priorities and needs is a basic requirement of a civilised society. If people understand and trust the system, they will feel increasingly free to get on with their lives without fear of crime, secure in the knowledge that there are opportunities for those who play by the rules and consequences for those who do not. But we also rely on public confidence to meet the practical needs of the system. We need the public to engage with the system by reporting crime and being willing to provide evidence as witnesses. And we depend on volunteers to support victims and to serve as magistrates or jurors.

3.1.2 Public confidence has increased in recent years. Improving the efficiency and effectiveness of the system builds on this. The Criminal Justice System must be more transparent and accountable to help the public understand how it is performing both nationally and locally. We must ensure we listen and establish a more dynamic interaction between the criminal justice agencies, the public and local organisations – business, voluntary bodies and community

groups – giving people a voice and opportunity to become active partners in the Criminal Justice System. This must be done in ways which build the confidence of all sections of the community that the system is fair and effective.

3.2 The story so far

3.2.1. Local, visible, accountable policing has an important part to play in building public confidence in the Criminal Justice System. Numbers of police and Police Community Support Officers (PCSOs) have increased. PCSOs, police and local authorities have the powers to tackle anti-social behaviour and disorder, helping to reassure the public. Since April 2007 there are now more than 12,000 Police Sergeants and Constables dedicated to Neighbourhood Policing across England and Wales. In addition, 16,000 PCSOs have been added to the extended policing family providing visible reassurance and tackling low level crime and anti-social behaviour.

3.2.2 We have established community justice centres in Liverpool and Salford to engage more with local communities. We are taking steps to make the wider work of the Criminal Justice System more visible and meaningful to local communities, to engage with those communities and respond to their local needs and priorities.

3.2.3 Community Payback has given local people, including victims of crime, the chance to say what work offenders should do: some seven million hours of unpaid work was carried out during 2006-07 by offenders making more visible amends to the public.

3.2.4 We are raising awareness and understanding of the Criminal Justice System with national campaigns such as "Inside Justice" and through the Justice Awards to celebrate the achievements of staff and volunteers. The Criminal Justice System is increasingly representative of the people it serves and all agencies have diversity plans in place.

CASE STUDY:

COMMUNITY PAYBACK - THE ALDERBROOK PROJECT

This was a Derbyshire Probation partnership with a day centre for adult learning difficulties. As part of community payback, offenders transformed a woodland area into a Woodland Wildlife Garden for the benefit of centre users. The work was primarily manual – constructing footpaths, laying hedges, building benches and carrying out pruning. Offenders learned skills needed by employers in the area. In partnership with Derby College 30 participants have achieved a City & Guilds Level 1 Amenity Horticulture Qualification. The success of the partnership has led to the day centre developing an on-site garden centre with the help of the Unpaid Work team. The project won the Environment Agency Award for Best Overall Project for Sustainability.

3.3 Our Vision and targets for 2011

3.3.1 Our vision is that people in local communities should be informed about the performance of the system, consulted and engaged about their priorities so they can be confident that it is fair, effective and meets local needs. Although public confidence that the Criminal Justice System is effective in bringing people who commit crimes to justice has risen, nearly 60% of people are still not confident that it is effective. The public think crime is going up when it is going down[6]. We must better communicate information about sentences and penalties to reduce public perception that sentencing is too soft: research indicates that when people are given the facts about the actual sentences handed out by the courts their confidence increases[7].

3.3.2 The Criminal Justice System must provide a fair and transparent service to all sections of the communities. A particular priority is to clearly identify and address any disproportionality in the service it provides to different minority ethnic communities[8]. Racial disparities within the Criminal Justice System still persist. Black people are seven times more likely to be stopped and searched and at least three times more likely to be arrested than white people[9]. 31% of people from black and minority ethnic communities think one or more Criminal Justice System agency will treat them worse compared to 11% of white people[10].

CJS / LCJB TARGETS TO SUPPORT DELIVERY OF OUR VISION FOR A CJS IN WHICH THE PUBLIC ARE MORE CONFIDENT AND ENGAGED

Justice for All PSA 2: increase public confidence in the fairness and effectiveness of the CJS

Justice for All PSA 4: consistent collection, analysis and use of good quality ethnicity data to identify and address race disproportionality in the CJS

The CJS and LCJBs also support Safer Communities PSA targets on:

Increasing public confidence in local agencies tackling crime and ASB

3.3.3 We need to increase better understanding and awareness of the Criminal Justice System and closer engagement and dialogue on performance with communities, users, volunteers and our frontline staff. For example, we know from surveys that staff satisfaction is rising but that they are less likely to speak highly of other parts of Criminal Justice System. We need to do more to help staff and volunteers see their role as part of a joined up service, not a single agency.

---

[6]Nicholas et al 2007.
[7]For example, Roberts and Hough 2005.
[8]We previously measured perceptions of fair treatment. We have moved to a more tangible measure of the extent of racial disparities in the Criminal Justice System. LCJBs will be required to collect and use improved and more comprehensive ethnicity data plus other diagnostic tools to identify, understand and address any unfair race disproportionality at key points within the system.
[9]Statistics on Race and the CJS 2006.
[10]Citizenship data April-June 2007.

3.4 Focus of action for LCJBs

3.4.1 We know that the key actions required to engage communities and drive up confidence are:

» providing regular and relevant information to communities about the performance of their local services;

» consulting them about priorities and local needs;

» taking action and providing feedback on what we delivered;

» addressing the needs of all groups, and particularly taking action to understand and address race disproportionality; and

» evaluating the outcome by measuring levels of public satisfaction and confidence in our services.

3.4.2 To build confidence and address potential unfairness across all parts of the system, LCJBs need to ensure that they collect and analyse good quality ethnicity data and have action plans in place when it is clear that there is disproportionality which cannot be justified.

3.5 The Partnership and Planning Framework for Local Delivery

3.5.1 Engaging effectively with local communities requires LCJBs to ensure that engagement activity across individual agencies is joined-up. As part of planning for community engagement we are asking LCJBs to ensure that individual agency initiatives are aligned and sequenced so that local people are asked once for their views and can see how the whole system works together. To support this work, the public confidence PSA target will be underpinned at LCJB level by indicators on staff engagement and community engagement.

3.5.2 LCJBs need to work collaboratively with CDRPs/CSPs whose mechanisms for community engagement are well developed[11]. At local authority level, delivery structures, activities and data exist, providing information on local perceptions of crime and the Criminal Justice System and enabling clearer identification of priorities for action. We are asking LCJBs and CDRPs/CSPs to agree shared local targets to increase public confidence drawing on all community engagement activity in the area.

3.5.3 As part of the Beacons Approach, OCJR has provided information on the core principles of community engagement. We will build on this and will publish in early 2008 an overarching Criminal Justice Community Engagement Strategy to support joint LCJB/CDRP/CSP work.

3.5.4 LCJBs will be asked to develop plans to address race disproportionality. Supporting this, we will provide more robust and accurate data to improve LCJBs' understanding of what is happening in their areas. We are introducing a basket of indicators to monitor the proportions of people from different ethnic groups at key stages of the Criminal Justice System.

[11]New regulations introduced in 2007 build on this by requiring CDRPs and CSPs to consult and engage with their communities to identify local crime and disorder priorities.

3.6 Nationally Driven Programmes and Initiatives

3.6.1 In drawing up their plans, local boards will want to be aware of the nationally driven programmes and initiatives setting the context for their work and on which they are able to draw to support local delivery, engage staff and communities and address race disproportionality.

Public confidence and community engagement: neighbourhood policing

3.6.2 Neighbourhood policing teams are key in strengthening engagement with communities and involving them in agreeing local policing priorities. Every community in England and Wales will have a dedicated neighbourhood policing team by April 2008. We will standardise our approach to ensure that all PCSOs have sufficient powers to support Neighbourhood Policing and tackle low-level disorder and anti-social behaviour. This will be supported with improved communication to increase public understanding of the role of PCSOs.

Public confidence and community engagement: prosecution and the courts

3.6.3 Although the police are the criminal justice agency having the most contact with the public, it is vital to build engagement across the Criminal Justice System so that the public understands and can engage with each part of the process. To support this, the CPS published a *Community Engagement Strategy* in 2006. The strategy includes a performance measure for community engagement. Community Involvement Panels will be set up at group level to engage community stakeholders, helping to inform and shape the service and enable the CPS to report on progress and account for its performance to the communities it serves.

3.6.4 Community Justice is about supporting the courts to engage with the local community, working in partnership with all criminal justice agencies, the third sector and community groups to solve the problems caused by offending in the local area. This includes strong case management, meeting communities to discuss their concerns and feedback on action taken. It provides opportunities for offenders to make visible reparation including using restorative justice where appropriate. Community justice aims to:

» make the court, visible, accountable and responsive to the community;
» break cycles of re-offending; and
» ensure that compliance with the court's orders or other penalties is seen and recognised by the community and that the community's problems are addressed.

3.6.5 Building on the North Liverpool and Salford Community Justice initiatives, we are working with LCJBs and other partners to extend community justice to eleven new court areas[12]. These projects will test different models of community justice in new locations around the country to help us then roll it out across all magistrates' courts.

Public confidence: 'Breakthrough' – improving services for all users of our courts

3.6.6 Achieving a breakthrough in performance for court users requires a step change in performance by court staff and other practitioners – police, prosecution, defence, probation, working with the judiciary and magistrates to provide continued leadership and drive. Court staff have drawn up eight key commitments to deliver simple, speedier and more effective justice across the Criminal Justice System and therefore a 'breakthrough' on the issues that matter to court users, whether family, criminal or civil cases[13]. These measures enable the development of benchmarks to assess court performance compared with similar courts and inspire all to meet the standards of the best. This will increase openness and enable the public to access information about the performance of their courts.

[12]These are Birmingham, Bradford, Devon and Cornwall, Hull, Leicester, London (Haringey, Newham and Wandsworth), Merthyr Tydfil, Middlesborough and Nottingham.
[13]The report *Delivering a Step Change in Performance: National Standards, Consistently Applied*, sets out how performance measures are being developed to test the delivery of these commitments.

CASE STUDY:

IMPROVING REPRESENTATION ON MAGISTRATES' BENCHES IN DERBYSHIRE.

Nigel Hallam, a Justices' Clerk in HM Courts Service in Derbyshire has worked tirelessly to improve black and minority ethnic representation on magistrates' benches across Derbyshire. His commitment to the Magistrates Shadowing Scheme has seen the percentage of magistrates from minority ethnic communities rise to a level which reflects the make-up of local communities. Having provided a role model to people who have come through the shadowing scheme and become a magistrate, he has encouraged them in turn to become role models themselves and the number of applicants from ethnic minority communities continues to rise. Nigel has gone this extra mile while still successfully carrying out his role as a busy Justices' Clerk. Nigel has now started to engage with the gay and lesbian communities to improve their representation on magistrates' benches in Derbyshire. Nigel received a Justice Award in 2006 for his work.

Community engagement – community payback

3.6.7 Community Payback gives local people, including victims of crime, the chance to say what work offenders should do in the community. Leaflets and websites inform people about particular schemes, making the unpaid work performed by offenders more visible and representative of communities' needs. Charities, community organisations and local authorities provide work places and benefit from the offender's contribution.

Community engagement – reducing re-offending

3.6.8 The three *Reducing Re-offending Alliances* launched in 2005 support delivery of national and regional plans to reduce re-offending. They do this by better informing, consulting and involving the public, with the private and voluntary sectors and local communities working with the Criminal Justice System to support ex-offenders to integrate into and contribute to society. These alliances are:

» **the Corporate Alliance,** which involves employers who are already taking on ex-offenders, promoting the case to others and helping ex-offenders to get sustainable jobs.
» **the Faith/Voluntary Sector Alliance,** which is building on the spiritual and practical help that these groups already provide for offenders; and
» **the Civic Society Alliance,** which promotes equality of access for offenders to mainstream local services such as accommodation and leisure facilities through improved partnership with local authorities and organisations and communities.

Addressing race disproportionality, raising confidence and tackling hate crime

3.6.9 To ensure public confidence in the Criminal Justice System we need to assure all communities and individuals that the system will treat them fairly. To support LCJBs in engaging with all sectors of their local communities, and in particular, increasing the confidence of ethnic minorities in the effectiveness of the Criminal Justice System, we launched the Confidence Toolkit in June 2007, and the Race and Confidence Challenge Fund for 2007-08. We will use the £250,000 Fund to support innovative, practical local activities increasing community engagement, increasing staff engagement, and increasing voluntary and community engagement.

CASE STUDY:

COMMUNITY ENGAGEMENT: HUMBERSIDE

Adil Khan is the manager for the Humberside Police diversity unit. His team includes a community race relations assistant and a hate crime coordinator. The team have built up strong relationships with groups of people in the community with particular needs who may be missed by 'mainstream' communications, such as asylum seekers, refugee communities, and gay and lesbian groups. They have organised five independent advisory groups across the police force area. These groups bring together all sections of the community including those most vulnerable, to improve the police force's understanding of the needs of particular groups in the community. The team arranges criminal justice open days for the public to improve their understanding of how the Criminal Justice System works. The open days have attracted over 800 attendees. In addition to this, Adil and his team advise the ACPO committees which tackle hate crime and address the particular needs of asylum seekers and refugees. As a result of this work, the force's critical incident training for community groups has received recognition as good practice and is being considered for use by all of the 43 police forces in England and Wales. Adil's team have received funding to carry out a study on why some people have low confidence in policing. They have also jointly, with the Grimsby Institute, developed and promoted a National Vocational Qualification level 3 in managing diversity which has been piloted within the force. His team are also involved in conducting 'mystery shopper' exercises to identify areas where the force can develop and improve and conducting satisfaction surveys on the quality of service delivered to support victims of hate crime. Adil's contribution led to him receiving a Justice Award in 2004.

3.6.10 We are implementing the Race for Justice Action Plan, aiming to improve the service offered to victims of hate crime by all Criminal Justice System agencies and support through:

>> the development of national occupational standards for dealing with hate crime;
>> independent training for the Judiciary on understanding and handling hate crimes; and
>> effective monitoring by criminal justice agencies through shared understanding, definitions and categories.

Communication

3.6.11 Our communications activity will continue to support LCJBs' community and staff engagement plans. We will continue successful campaigns such as the Justice Awards and opening up the Criminal Justice System through public facing campaigns.

3.6.12 An important part of this work is to increase public understanding of sentencing. We will support LCJBs to run local "You be the Judge" events. Members of the public get the chance to make decisions based on actual cases in magistrates' and Crown Court cases with real magistrates and judges leading proceedings.

3.6.13 Youth justice is a priority for our communications and engagement strategy. Only around a quarter of the public is confident that the Criminal Justice System is effective in dealing with young people accused of crime[14] and tackling youth crime is important to the public. Key to this is our drive to improve our response to youth crime and the efficiency and effectiveness of the youth justice process. We also need to ensure that the public and practitioners are more aware of the good work already underway in the youth justice system. The YJB is developing a communications strategy to support staff, the public and young people themselves. This includes supporting the dissemination of best practice in the youth justice system, encouraging partnership working including alliances between youth justice services and the voluntary sector, and supporting effective communication to wider audiences including through the local media.

[14]Nicholas et al 2007.

4 SERVING VICTIMS AND WITNESSES

High standards of service for victims and witnesses with the needs of victims at the heart of the system.

4.1 Why this matters

Victims and witnesses must be at the heart of the Criminal Justice System. This is important not only as a way of increasing public confidence, it is a fundamental part of why the system exists. No-one can undo the damage inflicted by the most serious crimes or the fear and distress caused by much low level offending and anti-social behaviour but through the Criminal Justice System, society can go some way to redressing that suffering. We must give victims a voice and ensure that offenders make amends to their victims and communities. It means tailoring the help, information and support provided to victims and witnesses. In particular, it means providing support and protection to the most vulnerable victims and witnesses, including children, and those with special needs.

4.2 The story so far

4.2.1 By setting service standards and improving our services we are responding better to the needs of victims and witnesses. From 2006, all police forces have been required to meet service standards set out in the Quality of Service Commitment. This helps improve ease of contact with the police, keeps victims informed of progress and engages with communities in developing services. The *Code of Practice for Victims of Crime* came into force in April 2006 assuring higher standards of support and information. Across England and Wales 165 Witness Care Units provide tailored, timely and practical

support with a single point of contact for witnesses from point of charge throughout the criminal justice process. Contact with victims by probation follows after a sentence where the offender in the case is serving 12 months or more for a sexual or violent offence, including mentally disordered offenders in certain circumstances. Prisons also provide a telephone helpline which victims can ring if they receive any unwanted contact from the offender or they have concerns about the offender's release.

4.2.2 Additionally we have pushed forward court improvements such as providing separate waiting rooms for witnesses and the friends and family of defendants. We have introduced a range of special measures to assist vulnerable or intimidated witnesses to give their best evidence in court, such as video recorded statements, giving evidence by live link from outside the courtroom and screens round the witness box so the witnesses cannot see the defendant[15]. We have established the Central Witness Bureau to support police forces providing witness protection and provided the National Witness Mobility Service, safely re-housing witnesses and their families in around 500 cases involving some 1500 individuals over the last three years.

---

[15]Independent research in 2004 on the effectiveness of special measures found that one third of witnesses would not have been willing to give evidence if special measures had not been available. Hamlyn et. al 2004.

CASE STUDY:

PROTECTION FOR VULNERABLE WITNESSES

Witness X, a 23-year-old woman from Eastern Europe, was the victim of a pan-European sex trafficking ring and had been sold into prostitution when she was a minor by her own family. She had been the victim of numerous brutal rapes and sexual assaults, bought and sold by three different trafficking rings and forced to work in brothels across several European countries. Witness X was granted asylum in the UK and was referred to the Central Witness Bureau by the police for safe and permanent accommodation. The National Witness Mobility Service (NWMS) in the Bureau quickly secured a flat for her. Her assistance to the police has led to the convictions of a large number of individuals across Europe. It is suspected that this prolific gang trafficked up to 500 women into the UK. With the intensive support of her dedicated police team and the safe and stable home that was found for her through NWMS, Witness X has been able to settle permanently in the UK and begin to put her traumatic experiences behind her.

4.3 Our vision and targets for 2011

Our vision is to deliver high standards of service to victims and witnesses with the needs of victims at the heart of the system.

We need to do more to embed service standards in all parts of the system from contact with police through to the payment of compensation. We need to look at the experience of victims and witnesses as a whole rather than just considering their interactions with individual agencies. There is more to do to meet the needs of the most vulnerable victims and witnesses. In particular, there is more to do to protect young people. Young people are particularly subject to repeat victimisation for violent crime[16]. We need to recognise the risk that some young victims of crime may go on to be involved both in offending and further victimisation[17]. We need to make best use of the skills and abilities of key partners, such as the voluntary sector, in supporting victims.

CJS / LCJB targets to support delivery of our vision for high standards of services for victims and witnesses with the needs of victims at the heart of the system

Justice for All PSA 3: increase victim satisfaction with the police and victim and witness satisfaction with the CJS

4.4 Focus of action for LCJBs

4.4.1 We know that the key actions required to raise standards of service for victims and witnesses are:

» **provision of the right information** to victims and witnesses at every stage, both on how the system works and how the case is progressing;
» **practical and emotional help** for victims that is tailored to their needs;
» specialist **support for the vulnerable and intimidated victims** throughout the prosecution process;
» a **voice for victims** and their families to express the impact of the crime on their lives; and
» **compensation** or reparation wherever possible.

4.4.2 In developing each of these areas, there is more to do to streamline the whole victim and witness experience. All too often individual agencies do not take sufficient account of the interactions that other agencies have already had with individuals. The same information can be requested more than once and standards of service can be inconsistent. We think that other agencies within LCJBs could learn from the experience of the Probation Service in supporting victims of some of the most serious offences and ensure that an integrated approach across the whole victim experience of the system.

---

[16]Wood (2005).
[17]Smith D (2004).

4.5 The Partnership and Planning Framework for Local Delivery

Locally the focus for planning and delivering service improvements in LCJBs will be the Witness and Victim Experience Survey (WAVES). This gives LCJBs and criminal justice agencies detailed local performance data on how satisfied victims and witnesses are with all aspects of the Criminal Justice System. Local areas may wish to supplement WAVES with other local data and sampling to understand, for example, more about the experiences of the victims of some of the most serious offences which are excluded from the current survey[18]. Using this data, LCJBs will be able to identify areas for improvement, working together with local partnerships through community engagement action plans. In the forthcoming planning rounds, we will be asking local boards to set local targets for improvement.

4.6 Nationally Driven Programmes and Initiatives

4.6.1 In drawing up their plans to improve standards for victims and witnesses, LCJBs will need to be aware of the nationally driven programmes and initiatives that set the context for their work and upon which they are able to draw to support local delivery.

Providing support to victims and witnesses

4.6.2 We will continue to develop the provision of practical and emotional support to victims and witnesses. Since 1997, our grant to Victim Support has risen to £30 million a year. In 2007-08 we provided a further £5.6 million to Victim Support to fund a programme of enhanced services for victims. We will work with Victim Support to ensure that their new enhanced operating model, providing direct, timely one-to-one support for victims, is embedded across England and Wales.

Through the Victims Fund we have invested around £7 million over the past four years into specialist support to victims of particular crimes. A majority of

this money (£6.5 million) has contributed to the £10 million package of direct specialist support for victims of sexual violence and childhood sexual abuse. We will continue to invest in specialist voluntary sector organisations that support victims and witnesses in more serious or traumatic cases, diverting money to them from offenders through the Victims' Surcharge.

4.6.3 We will improve the links between the voluntary sector and the Criminal Justice System. This will include better referral mechanisms from the police to Victim Support; improved arrangements for liaison and representation between Victim Support areas and LCJBs; and improved working between

CASE STUDY:

INDEPENDENT SEXUAL VIOLENCE ADVISERS

Independent Sexual Violence Advisers (ISVAs) work in a multi-agency setting to provide specialist advice and practical and emotional support to victims of sexual violence. They play an important role in supporting victims through the criminal justice process, as well as helping them to access the health care and services to which they are entitled. Some victims such as Jenny, who had been working in prostitution when she was raped, say that they would not have gone through with the court process had it not been for the ISVA. Gail, the ISVA based at St Mary's Sexual Assault Referral Centre in Manchester, supported Jenny through the video-interview, kept her informed about developments in the case and accompanied her when she gave evidence in court. The support she received gave Jenny the confidence to face her attacker in court and freed up valuable time for the police to get on with their job and build a strong case. Jenny proved a reliable and credible witness and the perpetrator received a 12 year prison sentence.

Victims withdraw in around 40% of rape cases and it is vital that we support them more effectively, through initiatives like ISVAs, if we are to improve the rate of offences brought to justice for serious sexual offences. We are formally evaluating the role of the ISVA, currently operating in 38 areas across England and Wales, with a view to wider roll-out.

---

[18]Victims of serious sexual offences are currently excluded from our measure of victim satisfaction with the Criminal Justice System for a number of ethical, methodological and practical reasons. We will be undertaking a feasibility study to see whether it is possible to address these issues so that we can actively monitor the experience of some of the most vulnerable victims in the Criminal Justice System in the future.

Victim Support, The Witness Service, Witness Care Units and Courts. We will also encourage local commissioning of the voluntary and community sectors and local partnerships between criminal justice agencies, the police, Victim Support, specialist organisations and, where relevant, health services, to ensure victims and witnesses' diverse needs are met.

4.6.4 We are working with LCJBs and wider local agencies to ensure a joined-up approach to addressing witness intimidation across the Criminal Justice System, building on the guidance we issued in 2006. We are continuing to roll out special measures to assist vulnerable or intimidated witnesses, including children, give their best evidence in court.

CASE STUDY:

SUPPORTING WITNESSES: LIVERPOOL

Mark Pathak, a social worker with Liverpool City Council's Investigations Support Unit works with witnesses who have a learning disability. The unit works closely with Merseyside Police and the CPS to ensure that people with learning disabilities are seen as credible witnesses. Since 1998 the unit's model of 'Witness Support, Preparation and Profiling' has helped 25 prosecution witnesses, usually victims of sexual abuse, to give evidence. The Witness Support Preparation and Profiling model involves working closely with a witness over a period of some 10-12 weeks. During this time the witness learns new skills and develops an understanding of the processes of giving evidence. At the end of this preparation stage, a Witness Profile is produced and served on the court. Mark has been involved in a total of 28 trials, 17 of which have resulted in convictions, three in acquittals, one mis-trial and one hung jury. The model has also been successfully used in six defence cases involving five defendants, and is now being implemented in different areas of the country. It is also being adapted for elderly people and for people with mental health problems. The unit has developed an "easy read" presentation of the model for adults with learning difficulties to understand using pictures and audio technology. Mark's contribution to supporting witnesses led to him receiving a Justice Award in 2004.

Video recorded statements, previously only available to children and vulnerable adult witnesses, were extended to adult sexual offence victims in the Crown Court from September 2007. We will be working with LCJBs to improve children's experience and interaction with the Criminal Justice System through developing toolkits that meet the needs of children and the local environment, complementing what is already in place. We are consulting on further ways to improve the criminal trial process for young witnesses.

4.6.5 The intermediary special measure provides support to vulnerable witnesses with communication difficulties. Following a successful pathfinder project in eight areas which has helped almost 800 witnesses, the intermediary special measure will be rolled out nationally in two phases and is expected to be completed by 31 March 2008.

CASE STUDY:

VICTIM INTERMEDIARY

In a case of wounding with intent the victim had suffered a brain injury as a child and now has communication and emotional difficulties. When he was unable to express himself properly, the victim would get frustrated and cry out in anguish or run out of the room. He also routinely answered 'yes' to questions. Without help he would have struggled to give an accurate, coherent and comprehensive account under cross-examination. To assist, the CPS obtained the assistance of an intermediary who assessed the victim and made recommendations about how to get the best evidence from him, including arrangements for taking breaks during questioning. At the trial the intermediary sat next to the victim throughout his live link testimony and provided assistance at appropriate times. The outcome was that the defendant was convicted and handed a life sentence. The CPS caseworker concluded that without the intermediary the case would have been lost.

Interpreters

4.6.6 There is a growing need for interpreters and translators in criminal proceedings. The OCJR has set up a project on interpreters:

» phase 1 led to a new National Agreement, published in January 2007, with advice on obtaining the services and standardising terms and conditions.

» phase 2 will identify measures to improve the supply. It includes measures to develop expertise, to explore the potential of technology to provide the services remotely and to engage EU support for such developments.

Service standards

4.6.7 We have already introduced minimum standards of service for victims under the **Victims' Code of Practice** and are now doing the same for witnesses through the introduction of the **Witness Charter**. In addition, the **Prosecutor's Pledge** will require all major public prosecuting authorities to take into account and protect the interests of victims at every stage of a case, in all types of case. A new CPS strategy for victims and witnesses will ensure that services are tailored to individual needs and targeted in the most effective and efficient manner.

Giving victims a voice

4.6.8 We will work to ensure that the right mechanisms are in place for victims to have their voice heard in their individual cases. For example, over two years to April 2008, a Victims' Advocate Scheme is being piloted in five Crown Court centres to give the families of murder and manslaughter victims an increased level of support before and during the trial and the option to read (or have read by the prosecutor or an independent advocate) a family impact statement out in court. Additionally, the CPS Victim Focus Scheme which commenced on 1 October 2007 is taking forward key elements of the Victims Advocate Pilots by ensuring that all bereaved families in murder, manslaughter (and additionally fatal road traffic cases) have the opportunity to meet with the prosecutor who will explain the charging decision, court process, the arrangements for making a victim's personal statement and to answer any questions the family may have. Following conviction, and before sentence, the prosecutor will offer to either read the statement to the court or invite the judge to read the statement in private according to the wishes of the family.

4.6.9 We will continue to work with the Victims' Advisory Panel so that our policies are informed by the views and experiences of victims themselves. Recent recommendations by the panel are helping to shape the way we improve services for victims and we will look to replicate this approach at a local level.

Compensation and making amends

4.6.10 No amount of compensation can ever undo the pain and distress caused to victims, especially in the most serious cases. However we are committed to improving compensation and reparation for victims and communities. For example, we are undertaking a radical reform of the way in which the Criminal Injuries Compensation Authority interacts with applicants, with the aim of reducing significantly the time that it takes to process a case, making the Compensation Scheme more focused on the needs of applicants.

4.6.11 Directly or indirectly, we will provide more opportunities for offenders themselves to make amends where appropriate. The Victims' Surcharge, which is being applied to fines in the courts, will go towards a fund to help improve services for victims of crime. Through the Conditional Caution, we are providing more opportunities for offenders to provide immediate compensation to victims in lower level cases and we are considering further ways to use restorative justice for minor offences in the youth justice system.

5 SIMPLE AND EFFICIENT PROCESSES

Simple, efficient processes – speedy, streamlined and efficient processes supported by modern technology that enable the police to focus their time on tackling crime.

5.1 Why this matters

Greater efficiency must always be a key part of the delivery of any public service. Delivering criminal justice efficiently, without unnecessary delay, will be the basis for improving every other aspect of the performance of the system. Improved efficiency will help drive up public confidence and improve the experience of victims and all those involved in the system as people see cases handled in a speedier and more streamlined way. And it will enable staff in every part of the system to focus less on bureaucracy and release resources for the things that will cut crime and protect the public. Critically, it will mean that the police can spend less time filling forms and more time on the street tackling crime. This means more modern working practices, supported by modern technology and by processes which are proportionate to the task. It also means making sure that there are alternatives to prosecution available to deal with uncontested, low-level offending, to free up court and probation resources for more serious and contested cases.

5.2 The story so far

5.2.1 As we set out in earlier chapters, we have delivered considerable performance and efficiency improvements to the Criminal Justice System. In the year to June 2007 we brought more than 1.4 million offences to justice and improved the charging process through the

CPS and police working together to get the charge right first time. The CPS now works at a much earlier stage in an investigation to identify the right charge and increase chances of success. "CPS Direct" supports the charging arrangements in all areas by providing an out of hours telephone service. A significant fall in the number of trials that fail to go ahead on the day has been achieved, saving thousands of pounds a day and hours of people's time.

Delivering Simple, Speedy, Summary Justice (CJSSS)

5.2.2 The CJSSS programme in the magistrates' courts is a new way of working in partnership across the system, bringing magistrates, district judges, defence, prosecutors, the police, probation and the courts together to make a real difference in tackling delay and improving efficiency. The aim is to improve the speed and effectiveness with which cases proceed and improve the way cases are managed. The four test areas in Thames, Camberwell, Coventry and West Cumbria saw significant improvements:

- » a large reduction in the time taken between first hearing and trial;
- » a 70% reduction in interim hearings between first hearing and trial;
- » a 24% increase in pleas at first hearing;
- » a 30% increase in guilty pleas at first hearing;
- » 59% of those pleading guilty are now being sentenced at first hearing; and
- » 70% of contested cases are now having just two hearings.

5.2.3 The overall ambition is to reduce the number of hearings in most cases from a current average of between five and six hearings to an expectation of one (for guilty pleas) and two (for contested cases). The majority of simple cases it is hoped will in future take on average between one day to six weeks from charge to disposal. The programe will be implemented across England and Wales by March 2008.

Technology to support efficient, joined up services

5.2.4 We have made major investment in improvements to Criminal Justice System technology and have largely delivered a modern IT infrastructure as well as many of the case management systems on which to build a more joined-up service to the public. For example, the CPS Witness Management System, delivered in 2006, is a single, national IT system which supports police and CPS witness care officers based in police stations in providing first class care for victims and witnesses.

5.3 Our vision and targets for 2011

Our vision is for speedy, streamlined and efficient processes supported by modern technology that

> **CJS / LCJB targets to support delivery of our vision for speedy, streamlined and efficient processes**
>
> Justice for All PSA 1: improve the effectiveness and efficiency of the CJS in bringing offences to justice

enable the police to focus their time on tackling crime. To achieve this we need to go much further in looking at the way the system operates as a whole. Too often improvements in one part of the system have simply resulted in bottlenecks elsewhere and so we need to co-ordinate our improvement programmes more effectively and make sure that changes in one area make the system work better as a whole. We know that we need to do more to make the best use of the technology which is now in use in every part of the system. Over the past five years cases have been taking longer, particularly due to an increase in the pre-court stage (offence to charge/laying of information at court). In particular as Sir Ronnie Flanagan's interim report on policing[19] set out, we need to take decisive action to reduce police bureaucracy freeing up their time to tackle crime.

[19]The Review of Policing – Interim Report (2007).

5.4 Focus of action for LCJBs and the Partnership and Planning Framework for Local Delivery

5.4.1 From our work with LCJBs we know that the key building blocks of a more efficient criminal justice process are:

>> more effective use of IT which is driven by the business requirements of frontline staff rather than IT professionals;
>> a clearer understanding of the end-to-end criminal justice process with clear data on the cost, timeliness, and effectiveness of processes;
>> a coherent and co-ordinated programme of change;
>> the capacity and capability needed to manage successful implementation of change.

5.4.2 Although the Beacon Approach is relevant to every aspect of service improvement, in its earliest stages it has focused particularly on efficiency. The support provided for the Beacon LCJBs is helping them to look at their processes as a whole in order to plan for improvement. For example, the work we have been doing with LCJB Beacons has included the development of an analytical tool, known as Waterfall, which provides a map of the standard Criminal Justice System process, and identifies areas of potential inefficiency. The process map can be used to overlay changes to business processes, providing a forecast of the value of the whole system benefits anticipated from Criminal Justice System reform locally.

Depending on what we learn from the evaluation of the Beacon Approach, we will be seeking to extend this support to all areas.

5.4.3 We also need to work with local boards on the development of the cross-Criminal Justice System measure of efficiency and effectiveness. We have already started work to develop a measure of cross-Criminal Justice System efficiency and effectiveness in bringing offences to justice. This will provide a high level measure which will allow us to demonstrate whether we have met the PSA commitment to improve efficiency and effectiveness. This will incorporate the implementation of the recommendation of Sir Ronnie Flanagan's interim report on his review of policing for a target to reduce bureaucracy by reducing the burden of case file preparation. Reducing bureaucracy is a national priority and we will be looking to each local board to deliver on this priority.

5.5 Nationally Driven Programmes and Initiatives

5.5.1 In drawing up their plans to improve efficiency, local boards will want to be aware of the nationally driven programmes and initiatives which set the context for their work and which they are able to draw on to support local delivery.

Freeing up police time

5.5.2 To free up police time, we will provide hand held computers so that officers can access critical information systems when they need them. They will be able to search local and national systems, record crimes on the spot, allowing them to stay on the beat and not waste time returning to the station to access IT systems or fill out forms. Mobile information devices are currently being trialled by six police forces in the UK, in conjunction with the National Policing Improvement Agency and other areas are independently taking up use of the device. Not only will this eliminate a massive administrative burden, it also ensures that information is up-to-date and accurate. By autumn 2008 we are aiming to provide 10,000 hand held computers across England and Wales and a £50 million fund has been made available to support this.

Simple, fair and efficient processes: postal charging

5.5.3 Postal charging is intended to reduce the administrative burden on police, prosecution and the courts in charging and launching criminal proceedings in lower risk cases. It will reduce the time between the end of the investigation and first hearing. It will allow the police to issue a written charge and postal requisition as a new method to bring offenders to court. This new method will replace the summons process, ending the requirement for a court to 'lay information' for a summons; and replace the face to face charging process (in relevant cases) where the suspect is released on unconditional police bail. We are rolling out pilots from 2007.

Simple, fair and efficient processes: case file preparation

5.5.4 Processes will be developed to ensure that there is a proportionate approach to case building to support the prosecution of minor crimes in the magistrates courts. This will reduce the burden on police of file preparation in those minor crimes where pleas of guilty are anticipated, and leave the police more time to devote to more serious crime, reduce the administrative burden on prosecutors and support CJSSS in speedy resolution of cases. A review will also take place in respect of the disclosure process (of unused material) in these cases to ensure that it operates efficiently with a minimum burden on Criminal Justice System agencies. This will further reduce the bureaucracy that police and prosecutors face.

Simple, fair and efficient processes: rolling out the CJSSS programme

5.5.5 The key to the success of the "Delivering Simple, Speedy and Summary Justice" (CJSSS) initiative in the Magistrates' Courts has been better inter-agency communication, better information available in advance and, more importantly, the development of a "right first time" culture. Through better preparation, the defence is in a position to advise clients properly and the court is able to ensure pleas are entered at the first opportunity. In contested cases, the court is in a stronger position to provide directions, identify key issues and fix a date for trial. We are taking forward a programme to implement CJSSS in each of the 360 magistrates' courts in England and Wales in 2007-08.

5.5.6 We are also working with the judiciary to introduce improvements in the Crown Court to achieve a reduction in the number of hearings and improve the speed and effectiveness with which cases proceed through the courts. The ambition is to reduce the number of pre-trial hearings from as many as six to no more than two in most cases and for the majority of cases to be disposed of within 16 weeks, except for complex and difficult cases. The current target is for 78% of committals and 'sent' cases to be commenced within 16 weeks.

Simple, fair and efficient processes: youth courts

5.5.7 We expect to apply the CJSS programme to the Youth Courts, subject to the results of a pilot programme at Balham Youth Court and taking account of the recommendations of an HM Inspectorate of Court Administration youth court inspection, published in March 2007. In support of our drive to join up and streamline our systems, we are taking forward "Wiring Up Youth Justice", a project to strengthen joint working and information sharing between YOTs and police.

Rewarding efficiency, not delay: legal aid

5.5.8 A legal aid reform programme was announced in November 2006 in *Legal Aid Reform: The Way Ahead*. A schedule of standard and graduated fees for defence lawyers is being introduced. This involves revised standard fees for magistrates' courts work in urban areas and a revised Crown Court graduated fees scheme for advocates; fixed fees for police station work which include travel and 'wait-in' payments; a new Crown Court graduated fee scheme for litigators; and phased introduction of best value tendering for police station and magistrates' court work.

5.5.9 The aim of these changes is to ensure that legal aid provision focuses on performance and outputs (case) rather than input (hours) and encourages speedy but fair progression of cases and greater continuity of representation in the early stages of a case.

Simple, fair and efficient processes out of court: Penalty Notices for Disorder and Conditional Cautions

5.5.10 Not all cases need to go to court. There is a range of lesser penalties and interventions from Penalty Notices for Disorder (PNDs) through to Conditional Cautions that can be used to deal with a minor offence simply, quickly and fairly to free up police time and reduce the burden on the courts.

5.5.11 The PND has provided police with a quick and simple "on the spot" response to low level offending by young people aged 16 years or over and adults[20]. We are carrying out a review to improve PND payment rates and

[20]We are evaluating pilots for issuing PNDs to 10 – 15 year olds.

fine enforcement. The national PND database (Pentip) which is due to be rolled out to all forces from March 2008 will help to address this. We are consulting on ways to improve the efficiency of the process for issuing PNDs so that they can be handled electronically using hand held devices.

CASE STUDY:

CONDITIONAL CAUTION – THEFT (BOURNEMOUTH)

The offender found a lost wallet in a supermarket. He initially meant to hand it in, but gave in to temptation and kept the money contained in it, discarding the wallet. He was seen to do so, and traced. The victim's main concern was the loss of a photograph of his late wife, which was in the wallet – he wanted some kind of apology. This was a first offence. The offender accepted a Conditional Caution, paying the victim compensation for his financial loss, and writing a letter of apology.

5.5.12 The Conditional Caution scheme has been introduced to provide a proportionate, swift and tailored response to low level, uncontested offending aimed at rehabilitating the offender and/or repairing the damage caused by the offending. They are used where sufficient evidence exists to prosecute the offender but the Crown Prosecutor assess that it is in the victim's and community's interest for the case to be dealt with outside the court process and the case is eligible for a Conditional Caution. Data provided by the CPS shows that by September 2007, nearly 4,000 Conditional Cautions had been issued, with victim compensation being the most frequent condition set. During 2007-08 we will continue to work with LCJBs to roll out the current Conditional Caution scheme nationally. In four areas, from autumn 2007 we are also piloting interventions to tackle alcohol-related offending through Conditional Cautions, as part of the Government's Alcohol Strategy.

5.5.13 Through the Beacon Approach we will be working with LCJBs to understand more about the volume and types of cases which may be suitable for a Conditional Caution, taking account of the impact of streamlining the court system through the CJSS programme.

Making better use of technology

5.5.14 We need to continue to make better use of technology in criminal justice processes. With the basic infrastructure, and many of the case-management systems now largely in place, we will now shift our focus on to supporting local boards in developing innovative ways of developing and using the technology they now have. Current national initiatives in development include:

» **Identity management:** we will improve the speed with which we can establish the identity of individuals coming into contact with Criminal Justice System, including identification of foreign nationals at the earliest possible point in the system. In support of our policy to deport those eligible for deportation as early in their sentence as possible, we are working with the Borders and Immigration Agency (BIA) to pilot a way to verify nationality at point of charge. This pilot will consider how a single identifier might be formulated to streamline the linking of information about nationality and identity of all individuals passing through the Criminal Justice System.

» **Improved data exchange:** We will speed up the entry of court results onto the Police National Computer (PNC) which will in turn speed up the sharing of data on dangerous individuals. We will continue to develop the "CJS Exchange" to share offender information between agencies. Through our "Wiring Up Youth Justice" programme we will strengthen the Criminal Justice System links across the youth justice system and strengthen its links with its wider partnership agencies to enable better risk assessment and early identification of those at risk.

» **Improved case management and preparation:** we will have more joined-up case management systems supported by effective information sharing across the Criminal Justice System. Improved case management will enable better risk and need assessments of offenders, such as those with complex substance misuse and/or mental health needs and ensure better management of compliance with programmes. It will also facilitate better monitoring to ensure public safety and the reduction of re-offending.

Better case management systems will enable better preparation for trials and sentencing. This will be supported through our multi-media strategy which aims to increase the capacity of the Criminal Justice System to use a wide variety of electronic media such as videos and digital evidence, to improve the efficiency of its processes (see below).

» **Understanding means and assets:** working in partnership with other government departments and agencies including Department of Works and Pensions (DWP), DVLA and HMRC, better systems for data exchange will ensure better and fairer means assessments and better and fairer targeting of means-tested legal aid. Better data exchange will also support more robust enforcement of fines and asset recovery measures and more efficient handling of motoring offences and confiscation and compensation orders. The Criminal Justice System will be better able to track offenders, their nationality and residency status, assets and their welfare status through the system to ensure their cases are dealt with both fairly and as rapidly and cost effectively as possible. This will mean that offenders will be identified and their needs and status assessed using information integrated from across the Criminal Justice System and linking up as appropriate with information from DWP, HMRC, DVLA, NOMS and the BIA.

Making better use of technology: multi-media strategy

5.5.15 Building on the IT systems we are also developing a multi-media strategy to further modernise our processes. This work has two main components, set out below.

Maximising the use of video conferencing across the Criminal Justice System

5.5.16 This programme aims to ensure that video conferencing is used across the Criminal Justice System, including the youth justice system, wherever it is the most effective and efficient means of carrying out criminal justice business. A national network of prison video links has been introduced to all local prisons so defendants on remand do not always have to go to court. Video links are in place in all Crown Court Centres and 77% of magistrates' courts, meeting our target to have video links in 75% of magistrates' courts by 2006.

5.5.17 We will be extending this capability to build video conferencing links with other parts of the Criminal Justice System, including probation, courts, police and prosecution and YOTs. For example, building on the principles of the CJSSS programme, we are looking to roll-out technology to support the creation of "virtual courts" for first hearings, building on a prototype for hearings that has been successfully tested in London where the defendant is dealt with at the police station. This includes the potential for defence lawyers to participate in the hearing on video.

5.5.18 This programme could significantly reduce delay between arrest and first appearance, free up staff time and improve services for victims and witnesses, including improved protection. There will also be benefits in reducing unnecessary travel, for example, reducing some of the costs of transporting prisoners to courts.

Electronic preparation and presentation of evidence

5.5.19 The electronic preparation and presentation of evidence programme aims to develop the system's ability to prepare and present digital evidence for trial hearings in high cost cases that are scheduled to take 26 days or more in trial time. It is estimated that these cases absorb over 20% of costs in the Crown Court but constitute less than 0.5% of cases.

5.5.20 Digital evidence can include any or all scanned documents, digital source documents, databases, spreadsheets, photos, CCTV footage, video and audio. Electronic presentation enables cases to be heard in court in a format that is quicker to present and easier to understand. We are finalising a programme of work which would aim to achieve at least a 30% efficiency improvement in such cases by extending the system's capacity to use digital evidence and enable the Criminal Justice System to keep pace with the growing volume and complexity of such evidence in the digital age.

CASE STUDY:

INTERNET AND MULTIMEDIA UNIT, AVON AND SOMERSET

The Internet and Multimedia unit, part of the Corporate Communications Department in Avon and Somerset police has specifically addressed the needs of the deaf community with the use of emerging internet video technology. They recognised that for some people, the internet was difficult because English is not their first language; and for others, they may use British Sign Language but cannot necessarily read and write English, even if they are from an English speaking family. Their website now features sign language video clips and subtitles. Information kiosks have been installed at shopping centres, park and ride facilities and other key community locations. These cater not just for the deaf community but are also wheelchair accessible and have speech facilities for anyone who is dyslexic, has poor eyesight or has learning difficulties. Initially the facility was only available in English and in sign language. The information kiosk facility has now added 14 languages.

The unit strives not only to provide a service which is of use to as many people as possible, but also to demonstrate respect for the deaf and other disabled communities as valued citizens in Avon and Somerset. As a result of their work, the team were highly commended in the Justice Awards in 2006.

6 HOW WE WILL DELIVER – NATIONAL FRAMEWORK, LOCAL DELIVERY

NCJB sets vision and high level targets

LCJBs define and implement local change

Closer partnership working between LCJBs, CDRPs and CSPs

National framework, local delivery – the National Criminal Justice Board will set the high level vision and targets for the criminal justice system with local boards increasingly responsible for designing and delivering the programmes needed to realise that vision. Local boards will work increasingly closely with Crime and Disorder Reduction and Community Safety Partnerships.

6.1 Why this matters – strengthening partnership working

The previous chapters set out the high level vision and direction for the Criminal Justice System and the targets that we will use to drive its delivery. Having strengthened performance and systems in all the criminal justice agencies, greater local flexibility and innovation is now the key to the next phase of joined-up reform. Increasingly local boards themselves will be responsible for designing and implementing the programme of change needed to deliver the key targets in our Public Service Agreement. To do that LCJBs will need to develop their capability to look across the whole system for which they are responsible and to plan for its improvement. Alongside that, LCJBs will also need to strengthen their ability to work with CDRPs and, in Wales, with CSPs.

6.2 Building the partnership between the National Criminal Justice Board and Local Criminal Justice Boards – the Beacon Approach

6.2.1 In July this year, we launched the Beacon Approach in ten criminal justice areas[21]. The Beacon Approach is not another change programme. It is a new way of delivering change. Through this approach, we will enable LCJBs to have a greater understanding of every aspect of their processes and performance and to develop an integrated and locally tailored programme of change and improvement. This means a new partnership between the NCJB and local boards. The NCJB, supported by the OCJR, will continue to be responsible for defining the vision and targets and for the high level policy framework within which the system operates. OCJR will provide the comparative and diagnostic data which will help areas to benchmark and improve their performance and efficiency and will share good practice. OCJR will bring national expertise to bear in developing innovative solutions, for example using modern technology, to the challenges faced by the system and will support LCJBs as they build their capability to take on an enhanced role in delivering local services. But it will be LCJBs themselves who will be increasingly responsible for defining and implementing an integrated local programme of change and improvement.

---

[21]The ten LCJBs selected to apply the Beacon Approach in 2007-08 are Cheshire, Cumbria, Greater Manchester, Lancashire, Leicestershire, London, Merseyside, Staffordshire, Suffolk and Thames Valley. These LCJBs are receiving support and training to conduct a detailed analysis of their criminal justice processes, using specially developed analytical tools. This will enable them to pinpoint the weaknesses and pinch-points in the way the Criminal Justice System works in their area, and to identify and prioritise the action needed to address them.

6.2.2 In this first phase, the Beacon LCJBs are implementing, as well as testing and refining, a core criminal justice reform programme designed by the NCJB, including major national change projects such as CJSSS in the magistrates' courts and Conditional Cautions (see below). It will also include PROGRESS, the case progression system which will enable case progression staff to manage offenders' compliance with the orders of the court.

6.2.3 The next step will be to evaluate the approach in the first ten areas. On the basis of that evaluation we will seek to extend the approach to other parts of the country. At present, this core programme largely comprises changes to improve the efficiency of the system and so as the approach develops we will seek to encompass changes to all aspects of the system.

6.2.4 In support of this approach, we are developing a new Criminal Justice Management Information System (CJMIS) which we rolled out in prototype in 2006. The system provides LCJBs with a single source of cross-CJS performance management information which is timely, high quality and locally-based.

6.3 Building the partnership between Local Criminal Justice Boards and CDRPs/CSPs

6.3.1 If we are to deliver our vision of communities engaged and confident and bring offences to justice in a way which reduces and re-offending, we need increasingly to bring together the work of LCJBs and the partnerships responsible for safer communities.

6.3.2 **National structures:** at national level, we are coordinating the Crime, Criminal Justice and Reducing Re-offending strategies through the NCJB working closely with the newly established National Crime Reduction Board (NCRB). These boards are supported by interdepartmental groups chaired by ministers on specific topics such as reducing re-offending. Together these boards will co-ordinate the work of government departments to deliver the wider criminal justice, crime and community safety targets, review overall progress and agree action to address risks to delivery.

Integrated planning process between local partnerships

6.3.3 The new Criminal Justice and Safer Communities PSAs provide the high level framework to enable LCJBs to work more effectively with CDRPs and CSPs. These contain two key outcomes that these two sets of partners share:

» **public confidence** – CDRPs/CSPs are responsible for building confidence that crime is tackled effectively and LCJBs are responsible for building confidence in the fairness and effectiveness of the Criminal Justice System.
» **building safer communities** – CDRPs/CSPs are responsible for work to reduce crime and re-offending and in particular for identifying and addressing local priorities. LCJBs make a contribution to that by focusing the resources of the system more effectively on serious crime and those local priorities so deterring crime and supporting the local crime reduction effort. They also provide opportunities for identifying and tackling some of the underlying causes of offending through the prosecution process so reducing re-offending.

6.3.4 It will therefore be increasingly important that LCJB and CDRP/CSP planning processes are more closely aligned. They should be based on:

» local partnerships developing a **shared understanding** of the needs of local areas and working together to **engage** communities;
» joint **planning and delivery** process for bringing offences to justice, focussing on **effective outcomes**; and
» **reviewing** progress and revising plans.

Developing a shared understanding

6.3.5 LCJBs can bring together the enhanced performance management data and tools provided at national level with the strategic assessments that CDRPs/CSPs need to provide on their local communities, using tools such as the police National Intelligence Model and the neighbourhood policing approach. LCJB data will include performance in bringing different types of offences to justice.

THE NEW DELIVERY LANDSCAPE

Nine Government Offices (GOs): provide a regional presence in England for central government and support increasing engagement between local partnerships. Reducing Re-offending Partnership Boards in the nine regions and a National Board in Wales include key representatives from the statutory agencies and the private and voluntary sectors. They support the national programme board and inter-ministerial group on reducing re-offending and develop action plans to drive forward local delivery. GOs also manage the performance of CDRPs and can support initiatives, consultancy and promulgation of good practice, and so can facilitate the relationship between them and LCJBs. A new Service Level Agreement between GOs and the HO and the MOJ is being developed. It will propose ways in which GOs may consider working with local partnerships through the new local performance framework. In Wales, there is a Home Office Crime Team in the Welsh Assembly Government, working in partnership with the Welsh Assembly Government's Community Safety Division, on the performance of CSPs in their delivery of plans for tackling crime and anti social behaviour.

Local Criminal Justice Boards (LCJBs): The 42 LCJBs in England and Wales were established in 2003 as non-statutory partnerships. They are based on police force and criminal justice areas. Membership comprises chief officers of the police, crown prosecution, court, prison, probation and youth offending services. LCJBs focus on improving the effectiveness of the CJS and supporting delivery of key targets and reform, working with the local partnerships set out below. The police serve on both LCJBs and CDRP/CSPs.

Local Strategic Partnerships and the Local Area Agreement: In England, local strategic partnerships (LSPs), which are non-statutory partnerships based on local authority areas, bring together the public, voluntary, community and private sectors to co-ordinate the contribution that each can make to improving localities by agreeing on the priorities and co-ordinating their delivery. *The Local Government and Public Involvement in Health Act* places a duty on local authorities to prepare the Local Area Agreement (LAA) in consultation with others. It also places a duty on the local authority and named partners to co-operate with each other to agree up to 35 local improvement targets for the LAA, derived from the single set of National Indicators. The LAA will form the main delivery agreement between central government and local government and its partners. In Wales, following the publication of the Welsh Assembly Government's response to the Beecham Review '*Delivering Beyond Boundaries*' and the local government policy statement: '*A Shared Responsibility*', work is progressing on the implementation of Local Service Agreements (LSAs). The intention is to have LSAs in place across Wales by 2010.

Local partnerships: Crime and Disorder Reduction Partnerships (CDRPs) in England and Community Safety Partnerships (CSPs) in Wales, were established in 1998 as statutory bodies bringing together the police, local authorities, fire and rescue and police authorities, and primary care trusts. There are 349 CDRPs in England[22] and 22 CSPs in Wales. Their aim is to reduce crime, fear of crime, anti-social behaviour, drug and alcohol misuse and environmental crime in their local area as part of the new local performance framework set out above. In England, in most areas, LCJBs will be liaising with CDRPs at county or unitary authority level. CDRPs are represented on LSPs through which the LAAs are negotiated and delivered.

6.3.6 To enable both LCJBs and CDRPs/CSPs to engage more effectively with the public, we need to ensure that best use is made of the information we collect about public opinion.

It is important that the public should not be faced with many similar survey demands. We are developing a new place-based survey to provide data on perceptions of crime as part of the new

---

[22] In England, those numbers are subject to change as the result of CDRP mergers and potential alterations to the structures of local authorities.

National Indicator Set. This will help create a more coherent system.

6.3.7 LCJBs and CDRPs/CSPs should take account of evidence about the most effective ways of reducing re-offending for certain crimes and information on local measures to tackle re-offending and reduce crime, including the demand and the capacity in their area for certain sort of interventions and treatment programmes.

Joint planning and delivery

6.3.8 On the basis of this shared understanding of the problems areas face and the issues that worry local people, LCJBs and CDRPs/CSPs will need to work together to plan an effective response. Their plans should set out:

» the strategic assessment of crime, and agreed local priorities;
» planned action to tackle those problems, based on strong evidence of what works. This includes a responsibility for LCJBs to produce a delivery plan which explicitly shows how it will support delivery of the Crime Strategy and the forthcoming Strategic Plan to Reduce Reoffending;
» how each partner contributes to the delivery plan; and
» identifying the resources required to deliver the plan, and how they have been allocated.

6.3.9 LCJBs and CDRPs/CSPs should meet regularly during the year to assess progress against plan, review performance, and take any remedial action they feel necessary. And they should review the plan annually to ensure that it remains valid and reflects community concerns. There are existing examples where LCJBs and CDRPs/CSPs are already working well together along these lines and we are drawing on their experience in developing best practice guidance.

CASE STUDY:

LEICESTERSHIRE LCJB TOOLKIT
The Leicester, Leicestershire and Rutland LCJB has supported the development of an overarching community safety programme board (CSPB) across the area. It brings together the criminal justice agenda of the local board and the community safety agenda of the CDRPs. The CSPB's key priorities include offender management, re-assurance and tackling anti social behaviour, drug and alcohol misuse. The CSPB was instrumental in establishing the Prolific and other Priority Offender (PPO) multi-agency delivery arrangements on behalf of all nine CDRPs in the area and more recently has supported the Civic Alliance Society national demonstration project undertaken in Leicester, Leicestershire and Rutland. This has resulted in the production of a toolkit for local authorities and other public service agencies involved in the work of CDRPs to help them contribute more effectively to reducing the risk of re-offending through enabling better access for offenders to services such as accommodation, employment and benefits advice, education and skills training, meeting health needs. This work will be taken forward locally by a new Reducing Re-offending Partnership Board reporting to the CSPB.

ANNEX A: DELIVERY OF OUR TARGETS 2004-08[23]

Improving public confidence **Reducing crime** **Improving victims' and witnesses' satisfaction**	» **Public confidence** that the Criminal Justice System is effective at bringing offenders to justice has risen from 39% in March 2003 to 41% in the year to March 2007. » We have delivered a 9% **reduction in BCS** crime in the year ending March 2007, compared with the 2002/3 baseline and a 42% reduction since 1995. » We are on target to reduce the number of people in **Black and Minority Ethnic communities** who believe the Criminal Justice System would treat them worse than people of other ethnic backgrounds. » **Victims and Witnesses** were satisfied with the Criminal Justice System agencies' handling of their case in nearly 60% of incidents in the year to March 2007.
Bringing more offences to justice	» There were over 1.4 million **offences brought to justice** in the year to June 2007, an increase of 43% since March 2002. » The **sanction detection** rate for the year ending March 2007 was ahead of target at 26%. » We have reduced the average time from arrest to sentence of **Persistent Young Offenders** from 142 days to 63 for the quarter to August 2007, ahead of our target of 71 days. » We are ahead of our 2006-07 targets to reduce the number of **ineffective trials** (i.e. unable to proceed on the day they were scheduled to start and re-listed to start another day) – performance currently stands at 12.2% (Crown Court, quarter ending June 2007) and 18.6% (magistrates' courts, quarter ending June 2007). » Through the **Witness Care Units** witness attendance at court has improved within the last two years from 77% to 84% as of September 2006. » The number of trials that did not go ahead as planned because a witness failed to attend has fallen by 13.6% in the magistrates' courts and 56.8% in the Crown Court since September 2005.

[23]Note: Full details of performance against target for 2006/07 and targets for 2007/08 are set out in the CJS Business Plan for 2007/08. The final report on our performance against our 2008 targets will be published in the CJS Business Plan for 2008/09.

Rigorously enforcing compliance **Reducing crime through reducing re-offending**	» We are dealing more effectively with defendants who fail to turn up to court – the number of outstanding **Fail to Attend Warrants** fell by 42% nationally between March 2005 and June 2007. By March 2007 there were 30,879 FTA warrants exceeding our target. » The **payment rate of fines** issued by criminal courts has increased from 74% in 2003-04 to 93% in the quarter ending June 2007 – ahead of our 83% target for March 2007. » Average time for resolving **community penalty breaches** is currently 42 working days, while performance in resolving breaches within 25 working days stands at 55% for the quarter ending June 2007. » In 2006-07 we achieved our target of recovering **£125m criminal assets**. » In 2006-07 the police/CPS secured 655 restraint orders and 3,335 **confiscation** orders to a value of over £85 million in under the *Proceeds of Crime Act 2002* and preceding legislation. » In 2006-07 the Revenue & Customs Prosecution Office (RCPO) secured 97 restraint orders and 445 confiscation orders to a value of £24.2 million under the *Proceeds of Crime Act 2002*. This exceeded their target of £22.7 million.
Joined-up and modern Criminal Justice System	» We have made major investment in improvements to **information technology** and delivered a basic cross-Criminal Justice System IT infrastructure. » We have built **strong partnerships** at national and local level. The Office for Criminal Justice Reform (OCJR) was set up in 2004 to co-ordinate joint policies and targets trilaterally across the Ministry of Justice, the Home Office and the Attorney General's Office. The establishment of the National Criminal Justice Board has strengthened trilateral leadership at the centre, while the 42 LCJBs have been fundamental to driving up performance at local level. » The Criminal Justice System employs a **workforce** increasingly representative of the communities it serves. » **The Criminal Justice System Departments** have set joint targets, developed joint policies and services on cross-agency issues like victim and witness care, defendants, charging and IT backed up by a joint performance management system. » **High standards of customer service across all Criminal Justice System agencies** are being delivered through the Victim Code of Practice and Witness Charter which set out how we hold agencies to account for meeting service standards for victims and witnesses.

ANNEX B: LIST OF ACRONYMS USED

ACPO	Association of Chief Police Officers
ASB	Anti-Social Behaviour
BCS	British Crime Survey
BIA	Borders and Immigration Agency
BCU	Basic Command Unit (policing)
CDRP	Crime and Disorder Reduction Partnership
CICA	Criminal Injuries Compensation Authority
CJMIS	Criminal Justice Management Information System
CJS	Criminal Justice System
CJSSS	Criminal Justice – Speedy, Simple, Summary programme
CPS	Crown Prosecution Service
CSP	Community Safety Partnership
CSPB	Community Safety Programme Board
CSR	Comprehensive Spending Review
CST	Community Safety Team
DCLG	Department of Communities and Local Government
DCSF	Department for Children, Schools and Families
DH	Department of Health
DIP	Drug Interventions Programme
DIUS	Department of Innovation, Universities and Skills
DVLA	Driver Vehicle Licensing Authority
DWP	Department for Work and Pensions
EU	European Union
FTA Warrant	Failure to Attend Warrant
GO	Government Office
HMCS	Her Majesty's Courts Service
HMICA	Her Majesty's Inspectorate of Court Administration
HMRC	Her Majesty's Revenue and Customs
HO	Home Office
ISO	Individual Support Order
ISVA	Independant Sexual Violence Adviser
IT	Information Technology
LAA	Local Area Agreement (England)
LCJB	Local Criminal Justice Board
LSA	Local Service Agreement (Wales)
LSP	Local Strategic Partnership

MAPPA	Multi-Agency Public Protection Arrangements
MARAC	Multi-Agency Risk Assessment Conference
MoJ	Ministry of Justice
NCJB	National Criminal Justice Board
NCRB	National Crime Reduction Board
NES	National Enforcement Service
NHS	National Health Service
NOMS	National Offender Management Service
NPIA	National Policing Improvement Agency
NWMS	National Witness Mobility Service
OCJR	Office for Criminal Justice Reform
PCSO	Police Community Support Officer
PNC	Police National Computer
PND	Penalty Notice for Disorder
PPO	Prolific and other Priority Offender
PSA	Public Service Agreement
PYO	Persistent Young Offender
RCPO	Revenue and Customs Prosecutions Office
SDVC	Specialist Domestic Violence Court
SFO	Serious Fraud Office
SGC	Sentencing Guidelines Council
SOCA	Serious and Organised Crime Agency
WAVES	Witness and Victims Experience Survey
YJB	Youth Justice Board (for England and Wales)
YOT	Youth Offending Team
YRO	Youth Rehabilitation Order

ANNEX C: LIST OF REFERENCES

Chapter 1

Cutting Crime, Delivering Justice. A Strategic Plan for Criminal Justice. 2004-08.

Comprehensive Spending Review 2007. Delivery Agreements for PSA targets.
http://www.hm-treasury.gov.uk/pbr_csr/psa/pbr_csr07_psaindex.cfm

All Wales Youth Offending Strategy. 2004.
http://www.yjb.gov.uk/en-gb/News/
AllWalesYouthOffendingStrategy.
htm?area=Corporate

Crime Strategy Cutting Crime – A New Partnership 2008-2011. July 2007.
http://www.homeoffice.gov.uk/documents/
crime-strategy-07/

Local Government White Paper 'Strong and Prosperous Communities'. October 2006.

Chapter 2

The Cross Government Action Plan on Sexual Violence and Abuse. 2007.
http://www.homeoffice.gov.uk/documents/Sexual-violence-action-plan

The Home Office National Delivery Plan for Domestic Violence. 2005.
http://www.crimereduction.homeoffice.gov.
uk/dv/dv017.htm

Criminal Justice and Immigration Bill. 2006-07.
http://www.justice.org.uk/images/pdfs/
CJIBsecondreadingcommons.pdf

Cross-government National Reducing Re-offending Delivery Plan. 2005.
http://www.noms.homeoffice.gov.uk/news-publications-events/publications/strategy/
reducing-reoffend-delivery-plan/

The Social Exclusion Unit's report on Reducing Re-offending by ex-Prisoners. 2002.
http://www.noms.homeoffice.gov.uk/news-publications-events/publications/strategy/
reducing-reoffend-delivery-plan/

Government Fraud Review Report. 2006.
http://www.attorneygeneral.gov.uk/
Fraud%20Review/Government%20Response%20
summary.pdf

Re-offending of adults: results from the 2004 cohort.
http://www.homeoffice.gov.uk/rds/pdfs07/
hosb0607.pdf.

The National Drug Strategy. 2002.
http://drugs.homeoffice.gov.uk/drug-strategy/

Asset Recovery Action Plan consultation document. 2007.
http://www.homeoffice.gov.uk/documents/cons-2007-asset-recovery/

Working with alcohol misusing offenders – A Strategy For Delivery. 2006.
http://www.probation.homeoffice.gov.uk/files/pdf/
Working%20with%20Alcohol%20Misusing%20
Offenders%20a%20Strategy%20for%20Delivery.
pdf

Corston Review of Women in the Criminal Justice System. 2007.
http://www.homeoffice.gov.uk/documents/
corston-report/corston-pt-1?view=Binary

Convicting Rapists and Protecting Victims – Justice for Victims of Rape: A consultation paper. 2006.

IPSOS-MORI. (2007). *Public attitudes towards Alternatives to Prosecution.* OCJR.

Cunliffe J. and Sheperd A. 2007. *Re-offending of adults: results from the 2004 cohort.* Home Office Statistical Bulletin 06-07 London: Home Office.
http://www.homeoffice.gov.uk/rds/pdfs07/
hosb0607.pdf

The Action Plan on Guns, Gangs and Knives. 2007.
http://press.homeoffice.gov.uk/press-releases/
tackle-gun-crime

Shapland, J., Atkinson, A., Atkinson, H., Chapman, B., Dignan, J., Howes, M., Johnstone, J., Robinson, G. and Sorsby, A. (2007). *Restorative justice: the views of victims and offenders. The third report from the evaluation of three schemes.* Ministry of Justice Research Series 3/07. Ministry of Justice.

Chapter 3

Community Engagement Strategy. 2006-09.
http://www.mpa.gov.uk/downloads/reports/
comengstrat06-09.pdf

Race for Justice Task Force Report. June 2006.

Roberts, J. and Hough, M. (2005). *Understanding public attitudes to criminal justice.* Open Berkshire: University Press.

Nicholas, S., Kershaw, C. and Walker, A. (2007). *Crime in England and Wales 2006/07.* 3rd Edition. Home Office Statistical Bulletin. London: Home Office Research Development and Statistics Directorate.

The Reducing Re-offending Through Skills and Employment: Next Steps. December 2006.
http://www.dfes.gov.uk/offenderlearning/uploads/
documents/Reducing%20Re-Offending%20
Through%20Skills%20and%20Employment%20
Next%20Steps.pdf

The National Delivery Plan for Hate Crime. June 2006. OCJR.

Statistics on Race and the CJS. 2006.
http://www.justice.gov.uk/publications/raceandcjs.
htm

Chapter 4

A Code of Practice for Victims of Crime. 2006.
http://www.cjsonline.gov.uk/the_cjs/whats_new/
news-3232.html

Witness Charter. 2005.
http://www.homeoffice.gov.uk/documents/
cons-witness-charter-2811

Smith D. (2004). *The links between victimisation and offending.* Edinburgh Study of Youth and Transitions. No 5. University of Edinburgh.

MORI. (2004). *MORI Youth Justice Survey 2004.* London.

Wood, M. 2005. YJB (Youth Justice Board) and HO (Home Office). *The Victimisation of Young People: findings from the Criminal Justice Survey 2003.* Home Office Research findings 246. London: Home Office.

Hamlyn, B., Phelps, A., Turtle, J. and Sattar, G. (2004). *Are special measures working? Evidence from surveys of vulnerable and intimidated witnesses.* Home Office Research Study No 283. London: Home Office.

Improving the Criminal Trial Process for Young Witnesses: A Consultation Paper. OCJR. June 2007.

Chapter 5

Legal Aid Reform: The Way Ahead. 2006.
http://www.official-documents.gov.uk/document/
cm69/6993/6993.pdf

The Government's Alcohol Strategy. June 2007.
http://horizon/crcsg/documents/Alcohol_all_
web.pdf

Flanagan, Sir Ronnie. (2007). *The review of Policing - interim report.*
http://police.homeoffice.gov.uk/news-and-
publications/publication/police-reform/The_
review_of_policing_inte1.pdf?view=Binary. 2007.

HM Inspectorate of Court Administration youth court inspection. March 2007.

Department for Constitutional Affairs. *Criminal Justice System. Delivering Simple, Speedy, Summary Justice.* July 2006.

Chapter 6

Local and Govt and Public Involvement in Health Act 2007.
http://www.publications.parliament.uk/pa/
cm200607/cmbills/016/2007016.pdf

Beecham Review 'Delivering Beyond Boundaries'. 2006.
http://new.wales.gov.uk/about/strategy/
makingtheconnections/beechamreview/
beechamrep?lang=en

Magistrates' court information on timeliness.
http://www.justice.gov.uk/publications/timeintervals.htm

British Crime Survey 2006-7
http://www.homeoffice.gov.uk/rds/bcs1.html

Crime in England and Wales 2006-07
http://www.homeoffice.gov.uk/rds/crimeew0607.html

Citizenship Survey 2005
http://www.communities.gov.uk/documents/communities/
pdf/452581

CJS online
http://www.cjsonline.gov.uk/

Crimes Detected 2006-07
http://uk.sitestat.com/homeoffice/homeoffice/s?rds.
hosb1507pdf&ns_type=pdf&ns_url=%5B
http://www.homeoffice.gov.uk/rds/pdfs07/hosb1507.
pdf%5D

*Crown Prosecution Service Annual Report and Resource
Accounts 2006-07*
http://www.official-documents.gov.uk/document/hc0506/
hc12/1203/1203.pdf

Revenue and Customs Prosecution Office Annual Report
http://www.rcpo.gov.uk/rcpo/about/rcpoar07.pdf

Printed in the UK by the Stationery Office Limited
on behalf of the Controller of Her Majesty's Stationery Office
ID5521985   11/07   19585

Printed on Paper containing 75% recycled fibre content minimum.